Cooking in a Casserole

Cooking in a Casserole

by Robert Ackart

Formerly published under the title
TO SET BEFORE THE KING

GROSSET & DUNLAP
A National General Company
Publishers   New York

Copyright © 1967 by Robert C. Ackart
All rights reserved
Published simultaneously in Canada

Formerly published under the title TO SET BEFORE THE KING
First published in 1973 under the title COOKING IN A CASSEROLE,
by Grosset & Dunlap, Inc.
Printed in the United States of America

Illustrations by Marjorie Zaum

*For Gene Boucher,
taster and critic,
with affection*

Contents

Foreword	11
Fact and Opinion—Items to Help the Cook	15

Part I

The Main Dish	19
Meats	21
Poultry	141
Fish and Seafood	185
Soups and Soup-Stews	227

Part II

A Few Companionable Side Dishes	249
Rice, Barley, and Bulgur	251
Vegetables	258
A Few Salads	275
A Few Breads and Muffins	293
Desserts	303
A Few Drinks and Appetizers	319
Index	333

Cooking in a Casserole

FOREWORD

The novelty of this cookbook lies, I believe, in its offering over one hundred main dishes of different nationalities, each cooked and served in a single utensil, accompanied by menus for the complete meal.

The main dishes are devoted to meats, poultry, fish, and soup-stews. Side dishes of rice, barley, and bulgur are followed by ideas on cooking vegetables and by a few vegetable recipes. Some general notions about salads are given, together with some specific recipes for them and their dressings. Five recipes for breads and their several possible variations, eleven desserts, and a final section on a few drinks and appetizers complete the book. The number of side dishes is purposely limited for the convenience of the cook. Recipes for the side dishes are listed in the index under their particular names. All the recipes, like a deck of cards, may be shuffled in various combinations; their use is not dictated by the menus as given.

Suggestions are made for serving wine. The ideas are confined to *types* of wine which I find go well with particular dishes. Information on vineyards, brands, and names is best had from a wine-merchant who can accommodate the choice of wine to your personal preference and pocketbook.

So that the reader may jot down ideas on the main dish, menu, and wine, space for notes is provided with each main dish recipe.

Several recipes, even some "national" ones, are my inventions (and are so marked in the French manner—"Seafood Stew—*Maison*"). Many are contributions from friends who enjoy cooking and good food; some derive from places where I have eaten. Recipes which have not been begged, borrowed, or stolen from friends, relations, and restaurants, have come from various publications,

Foreword

and from old and new books; all have been adapted to available ingredients which can be easily prepared from an immediately-read format and with a minimum of utensils.

To add interest to the dishes, their nationality is given. I believe most geographical sources are accurate; sometimes, however, when unable to identify the native land, I have ascribed a nationality to the dish by reference to the character of its ingredients. I find a meal with dishes from different lands as interesting as, for example, an entirely Italian or exclusively Middle Eastern one. Hence the menus are not necessarily geographically oriented—albeit many are—but evolve from food combinations which go well together. The one-country or regional menu brings together a full meal characteristic of a single area or culture.

The recipes are written to serve six persons; the possibilities of doubling for larger groups are indicated (and if a recipe may be doubled, it often may be tripled or quadrupled), as is the feasibility of refrigerating or freezing. Finally, the time required to make the recipe is divided into preparation- and cooking-time; these timings are approximate, depending upon the speed of the cook, the organization of the kitchen, and so forth.

In preparing the main dish, a 6-quart casserole is used almost exclusively, for both on-the-stove and oven cooking. (Whenever possible, I prefer the oven; its heat tends to be steadier and it makes for less clutter in the kitchen.) Do not misunderstand what is meant by cooking with casserole: I deplore baked tuna-and-noodles! I applaud, however, the casserole as a *method* of cooking, particularly when—as is intended here—the method can be applied to many different kinds of dishes prepared with facility.

Other than the 6-quart casserole or baking dish, no special equipment is necessary in the preparation of these meals. Some recipes require an electric blender—a boon to the modern cook—and if you do not have one, I cannot urge strongly enough its purchase. What is indispensable in my kitchen is a battery of herbs and spices with which I experiment constantly (and when something *good* happens, I write it down).

About ingredients: at the beginning of each section (on beef, on lamb, on poultry, and so forth) some general comment is made on the selection of the main ingredient. These suggestions, it is hoped, will make things easier for the cook. In addition, however,

Foreword

it should be remembered that no completed dish is better than its individual constituents: poor quality meat or tough poultry will yield a less satisfying meal, no matter how skillfully prepared, than will first-rate ingredients.

My special thanks to Marjorie Zaum for the pleasure and privilege of working with her on the book and to my neighbor Ellen Fagergren for help in correcting galley proofs.

Enough of Foreword! Forward now to an enjoyable use of this book and to the pleasurable meals I hope you make from it!

Robert Ackart

FACT AND OPINION

Items intended to help the cook (alphabetically arranged)· *"At this point you may stop and continue later"*: this direction will be useful to the cook unable to complete the recipe at one time or who prefers not to warm up the completed casserole. When cooking is resumed, bring the dish to heat (usually simmering) before continuing with the next step of the recipe.

Bouillon: when chicken or meat broth or bouillon (or consommé) is called for, reference is made to the standard size of canned soups. Canned broth and bouillon are richer and more flavorful than that made from cubes or powder. The latter, however, are very useful in cooking rice and vegetables and may be substituted in all recipes for the canned variety.

Butter: butter is specified in these recipes, but margarine or a combination of butter and margarine may be used.

Canned goods: if you substitute canned ingredients for fresh, remember that a 1-lb. can equals approximately 2 cups and serves 3 or 4 persons. Reserved vegetable water may be used as part of the liquid ingredient of the recipe. Canned vegetables, already cooked, should be added to the recipe only long enough to heat through. As is the case with frozen ingredients, use of canned goods necessitates adjustments of timing.

Fact and Opinion

Some sizes of cans:

fruits	⎫
onions	⎪
potatoes	⎬ 1-lb. can
sauerkraut	⎪
tomatoes	⎪
tomato sauce	⎭

mushrooms	⎰ small 3- or 4-oz. can
	⎱ large 6- or 8-oz. can
tomatoes	also available in 1-lb. 12-oz. can
tomato paste	6-oz. can

Casserole: a 6-quart enamelized-iron casserole is recommended; it works well for either top-of-stove or oven cooking, is the most easily cleaned, and will not affect wine cookery (see below, under "Wine").

Oven-proof, flat baking dishes of up to 2-quart capacity are useful for some recipes, particularly fish dishes, but are not essential.

A small 3-quart enamelized-iron casserole is convenient for cooking rice, barley, or bulgur.

Doubling: possibilities for recipe doubling are indicated at the upper right of each entry. If doubling is not practical, the word "doubles" is omitted; if I have reservations about it, I say why.

Eggplant: use of this fruit—for such it is, botanically speaking—is an important contribution from the Middle East to occidental cookery. A large eggplant—usually called for here—weighs about 2 lbs. Unless peeling is suggested, do not.

Freezing: if your freezer will not accommodate a 6-quart casserole, use as many freezer containers as necessary. Do not freeze until dish has cooled to room temperature. Allow to thaw to room temperature before reheating, gently. If you freeze dish before recipe is completed, bring thawed casserole to heat (usually simmering) before continuing with next step of recipe.

Frozen ingredients: whenever available I prefer fresh ingredients, but when time prohibits their preparation, I use frozen ones—chopped onion, chopped pepper, mushrooms, parsley, chives, as

Fact and Opinion

well as standard garden vegetables. Cooking with frozen ingredients differs from that with fresh; it is almost impossible, for example, to glaze or to cook until golden chopped or whole frozen onion because of the water content which freezing-thawing produces; therefore the cook will have to adjust his timing and methods. The standard frozen food package called for in these recipes weighs 10 oz.; exceptions are green beans and artichoke hearts (9 oz.) and yellow squash (12 oz.).

Fruits: the use of fruit in combination with meat is, I am told, typical of the Middle East and Orient. It is not in general practice among occidental cooks, but should be. If dried fruit is called for, use the packaged variety available at your supermarket; if canned fruit is needed, buy the 1-lb. can and allow for two cans, drained, to yield about 3 cups.

Margarine: may be used in place of butter in these recipes, or a combination of the two.

Marinating: I find that lengthening the designated marinating time a bit never hurts; cutting it short frequently robs the completed dish of flavor or tenderness. Marinating may be done in or out of the refrigerator; my feeling, entirely personal, is that in-the-refrigerator marinating is less effective than allowing the ingredients to bathe in their marinade at room temperature.

Oil: unless otherwise specified, I use a mixture of half olive and half corn oils for both cooking and salads. Use of olive oil alone makes for a heavy taste; combining the two prevents this. To assure against butter burning when browning meat or vegetables, I often add 1 or 2 Tbs corn oil to the casserole.

Oven and top-of-stove cooking: as suggested in the Foreword, I prefer oven cooking as being steadier in heat, cleaner, and less cluttering to the small modern kitchen. I have prepared such of these recipes as permit both *in* and *on* the stove and find that both methods work and both require about the same amount of time. Many stoves now have a "thermal eye" which allows of careful regulation of top-of-stove cooking. The success of cooking *en casserole* lies in a slow, simmering, even heat, so that flavors meld and meat ingredients tenderize. Fish cookery is the exception to

Fact and Opinion

this rule—for which directions are given in the section on fish and seafood.

Parsley: is available in three forms—fresh, dried, and frozen. Fresh is preferable and usually available. Dried is the best substitute, I feel; frozen parsley tends to be watery, but is good to stir in at the last minute when it gives flavor without cooking.

Pepper: of the three popular peppers—black, white, and red—black is the one called for unless otherwise stipulated. White pepper is the same as black save that the dark hulls have been removed; it is used when flavor but not color is desired. Red pepper, quite different from paprika, is never used without being specifically suggested.

Refrigerating: is best done in the casserole in which the recipe is prepared (saves washing up); if your refrigerator will not accommodate a 6-quart casserole, use whatever will fit. If you refrigerate mid-way in the preparation of a dish, the casserole should reach room temperature and then be brought to heat (usually simmering) before you continue with the recipe. Completed recipes, refrigerated, should reach room temperature before being gently reheated (to prevent overcooking).

Wine: Recipes prepared with wine should be cooked in an enamelized-iron casserole; otherwise, the wine will pick up the metallic taste of the utensil. When "1 bottle of wine" is called for, the standard litre measure is intended. I keep both red and white wine on hand at all times—even if the given recipe does not call for wine, the dish is most frequently improved by its addition.

There is no such thing as "cooking wine." There is only good and less-good wine, and while it is unnecessary to cook with wine of rare vintage, your palate will convince you that the quality of the dish reflects the quality of the wine used in it.

Part One
THE MAIN DISH

Main Dishes made with Meats

As suggested in the Foreword, an enamelized-iron casserole is recommended—by far the easiest to clean. Meats prepared *en casserole* benefit from advance cooking. The flavors mellow and meld. The meat tenderizes a bit more. And, if the dish is refrigerated or frozen, excess fat may be readily removed and discarded. Refrigerated or frozen dishes should be at room temperature before being gently reheated, covered (300° for 30 to 45 minutes); this precaution prevents overcooking.

Casseroles made with Beef

For many people, stew, like bread and butter, is a "staff of life." Families struggling with food budgets eat it often. Many party-givers rely on it as a tasty way of feeding guests. Most important, people who like good food enjoy it. Beef stews can and should be distinctive; often, however, meat and accompanying ingredients are allowed to lose their identity through overcooking or indiscriminate flavor combinations. The resultant mush is—just that! I think the following beef stews have individuality, and for them recommend lean chuck cut into bite-size pieces, about 1½" cubes.

Recipes for the suggested side dishes given with each main dish may be found elsewhere in the book.

BEEF WITH BEER AND HERBS (*Flemish*)

Serves 6
Doubles
Refrigerates
Freezes

TOTAL TIME:
about 3¼ hours
(45 minutes preparation,
2½ hours cooking)

You will need . . .

¼ lb. thick-sliced bacon, diced
3 lbs. beef (page 23)
1 tsp salt
4 onions, chopped

2 Tbs butter
2 Tbs flour
1 12-oz. can warm beer
1 tsp salt
½ tsp each:
pepper, marjoram, thyme, rosemary
1 tsp sugar
1 clove garlic, minced

2 Tbs cider vinegar
Reserved bacon

Serve with . . .
muffins (American)
salad with dressing
peaches with red wine
(French)
Wine suggestions:
vin rosé, domestic
Burgundy

24

BEEF WITH BEER AND HERBS (*Flemish*)

Preparation . . .

1. Assemble and prepare all ingredients.
2. In 6-quart casserole, render bacon until crisp; remove to absorbent paper and reserve. In remaining bacon fat, brown meat; season with salt. Add onions and continue to cook, stirring, until onions are translucent.

    At this point you may stop and continue later.

3. In saucepan, melt butter and add flour, stirring to blend. Add beer, stirring, and bring to boil; add seasonings. When sauce is thick and smooth, add to casserole and stir.

Cooking . . .

4. Cook casserole, covered, at 300° for 2½ hours, or until meat is tender. More beer may be added if necessary.
5. Just before serving, stir in vinegar and garnish with reserved bacon.

BEEF BRISKET WITH VEGETABLES (*French*)

Serves 6
Doubles
Refrigerates

TOTAL TIME:
about 3½ hours
(*30 minutes preparation,
3 hours cooking*)

You will need . . .

4 lbs. brisket of beef
¾ lbs. salt pork
1 marrow bone
2 onions, stuck with cloves
3 leeks, washed and sliced
(6 sliced scallions will do)
2 carrots, sliced
Water

2 bay leaves, crushed
1 tsp thyme
1 tsp salt
1 tsp sugar
¼ tsp pepper

Better known as pot au feu, *this casserole is a classic one-dish meal.*

6 onions, peeled
6 leeks (or scallions)
washed and sliced
6 carrots, sliced
6 small turnips, sliced
1 small cabbage,
cut in 6 portions

Serve with . . .
bread *en casserole* (*French*)
individual chocolate mousse
(*French*)
Wine suggestions:
red Bordeaux,
domestic claret

BEEF BRISKET WITH VEGETABLES (*French*)

Preparation . . .

1. Assemble and prepare all ingredients.
2. In 6-quart casserole, combine first six ingredients; add water to cover 1½" above meat. Boil rapidly for 5 minutes; remove from heat, skim.

Cooking . . .

3. Add seasonings and bring to second boil; reduce heat and simmer, covered, for 2 to 2½ hours, or until meat is tender.

    At this point you may stop and continue later.

4. Remove meat to 250° oven. Add the first four vegetables to meat stock; boil for about 20 minutes, or until vegetables are just tender.
5. Add cabbage and cook 15 minutes longer.
6. To serve, slice brisket and salt pork; arrange on platter and surround with vegetables. Garnish with marrow from marrow bone. If desired, serve broth in cups.

BEEF WITH BURGUNDY (*French*)

---

*Serves 6 generously
Doubles
Refrigerates
Freezes*

TOTAL TIME:
*about 3 hours
(30 minutes preparation,
2½ hours cooking)*

You will need . . .

4 Tbs oil
¼ lb. salt pork, diced
6 carrots, sliced
4 lbs. beef (page 23)
Salt
Pepper
Sugar
2 cloves garlic, minced
6 onions, chopped
1 lb. mushrooms, rinsed and sliced

The classic boeuf bourguignonne is perhaps the most celebrated of beef stews.

1 bottle red burgundy
⅔ cup cognac

Serve with . . .
bread en casserole (*French*)
spinach salad (*French*)
individual chocolate mousse (*French*)
Wine suggestions:
red Côtes du Rhone,
domestic claret

BEEF WITH BURGUNDY (*French*)

Preparation . . .

1. Assemble and prepare all ingredients.
2. In 6-quart casserole, heat oil slightly and spread evenly over bottom and sides. Arrange in layers ½ the salt pork, all the carrots, and ⅓ the beef. Sprinkle with salt, pepper, and a pinch of sugar.

   Add, in layers, ½ the onions, ½ the garlic, ½ the mushrooms, and ⅓ the beef. Sprinkle with salt, pepper, and a pinch of sugar.

   Add, in layers, remaining onions, garlic, mushrooms, and beef. Sprinkle with salt, pepper, and a pinch of sugar.

   At this point you may stop and continue later.

Cooking . . .

3. Pour over wine and cognac. Bring casserole rapidly to boil; reduce heat and simmer, covered (liquid should barely bubble), for 2½ hours, or until meat is tender.
4. To reduce liquid, remove cover and continue to simmer.

BEEF WITH CURRANTS (*Greek*)

Serves 6
Doubles
Refrigerates
Freezes

TOTAL TIME:
*about 3 hours
(30 minutes preparation,
2½ hours cooking)*

You will need . . .

3 lbs. beef (page 23)
1 tsp salt
¼ tsp pepper
4 Tbs butter
18 small onions, peeled
1 can tomato paste

½ cup dry red wine
2 Tbs wine vinegar
1 clove garlic, minced
1 bay leaf, broken
1 2″ piece cinnamon stick
½ tsp whole cloves
½ tsp ground cumin
⅓ cup currants (or raisins)

Serve with . . .
bulgur (Middle Eastern)
salad with dressing
and feta cheese
dried fruit compote
Wine suggestions:
red Burgundy,
domestic claret

BEEF WITH CURRANTS (*Greek*)

Preparation . . .

1. Assemble and prepare all ingredients.
2. Season meat with salt and pepper. In 6-quart casserole, melt butter and add meat, stirring to coat well—do not brown.
3. Add onions and tomato paste.

    At this point you may stop and continue later.

4. Combine wine, vinegar, and garlic; pour over casserole. Add seasonings and currants.

Cooking . . .

5. Cook, covered, in 300° oven for 2½ hours, or until meat is tender.

BEEF WITH CURRY (*Middle Eastern*)

Serves 6
Doubles
Refrigerates
Freezes

TOTAL TIME:
about 6 hours
(*30 minutes preparation,*
3 hours marinating,
2½ hours cooking)

You will need . . .

2 cups yoghurt
2 onions, chopped
2 cloves garlic
2 Tbs ground coriander
2 tsp ground ginger
2 tsp turmeric
1 tsp salt
1 tsp sugar
1 tsp cinnamon
1 tsp ground cumin
½ tsp crushed red pepper flakes
1 dash cayenne

3 lbs. beef (page 23)
2 Tbs oil

3 cloves garlic, minced
2 onions, chopped

Serve with . . .
rice
salad with dressing
jellied sherry (Spanish)
Wine suggestions:
domestic or imported
vin rosé

32

BEEF WITH CURRY (*Middle Eastern*)

Preparation . . .

1. Assemble and prepare all ingredients.
2. In container of electric blender, combine the first twelve ingredients and blend for 20 seconds at low speed.

3. In yoghurt-spice mixture, marinate meat for 3 hours.
4. In 6-quart casserole, heat oil; add garlic and onions and cook until translucent.

At this point you may stop and continue later.

Cooking . . .

5. Add meat and marinade to casserole and simmer, covered, for 2½ hours, or until meat is tender.
6. Remove cover, bring to boil, and reduce liquid to a thick sauce.

GROUND BEEF WITH EGGPLANT (*Italian*)

Serves 6
Doubles
Refrigerates
Freezes

TOTAL TIME:
about 1 hour
(30 minutes preparation,
30 minutes cooking)

You will need . . .

1 large eggplant, cut in ½" slices

6 slices bacon, diced
1 green pepper, chopped
1 onion, chopped
1 clove garlic, minced
2 lbs. ground round

2 cups canned Italian tomatoes
1 can tomato paste
1 tsp oregano
1 tsp salt
¼ tsp pepper
2 Tbs flour
2 Tbs water

Grated Parmesan cheese

Serve with . . .
bulgur (Middle Eastern)
salad with dressing
pears with curry
(Middle Eastern)
Wine suggestions:
red Bordeaux,
domestic claret

GROUND BEEF WITH EGGPLANT (*Italian*)

Preparation . . .

1. Assemble and prepare all ingredients.
2. In salted boiling water, cook eggplant for 5 minutes; drain.
3. In 6-quart casserole, render bacon until crisp; drain and reserve. In remaining fat, cook pepper, onions, and garlic until onion is translucent. Drain off excess fat. Add meat and brown.

At this point you may stop and continue later.

4. Combine tomatoes, tomato paste, and seasonings. Mix flour and water until smooth and add to sauce. Add meat mixture, stirring to blend.

Cooking . . .

5. In casserole, arrange alternate layers of eggplant and meat mixture. Top with reserved bacon bits and grated cheese. Bake, uncovered, at 350° for 30 minutes.

BEEF WITH FRUIT—MAISON (*American*)

Serves 6
Doubles
Refrigerates
Freezes

TOTAL TIME:
about 3¼ hours
(45 minutes preparation,
2½ hours cooking)

You will need . . .

2 lbs. beef (page 23)
¼ cup flour
1½ tsp salt
½ tsp pepper
3 Tbs oil
2 cloves garlic, chopped
3 onions, chopped

3 cups beef bouillon
1 tsp marjoram
½ tsp ground allspice
1 tsp sugar

3 carrots, thinly sliced
3 stalks celery, chopped
1 green pepper, chopped
18 dried prunes (pitted, if available)
1 cup dried apricots

Serve with . . .
muffins (*American*)
water cress and
mushroom salad (*American*)
sponge pudding (*American*)
Wine suggestions:
domestic or imported
vin rosé

BEEF WITH FRUIT—MAISON (*American*)

Preparation . . .

1. Assemble and prepare all ingredients.
2. Dredge meat in flour seasoned with salt and pepper. In 6-quart casserole, heat oil; add meat and brown. Add garlic and onion and cook until translucent.

   At this point you may stop and continue later.

Cooking . . .

3. Add bouillon and seasonings, bring casserole to boil; reduce heat and simmer, covered, for 2 hours, or until meat is just tender.

   At this point you may stop and continue later.

4. Add remaining ingredients, stir gently and continue to simmer, covered, for 20 to 30 minutes, or until vegetables and fruit are tender.

BEEF WITH GINGER (*Burmese*)

*Serves 6
Doubles
Refrigerates
Freezes*

TOTAL TIME:
*about 7 hours
(30 minutes preparation,
4 hours marinating,
2½ hours cooking)*

You will need . . .

6 medium onions, chopped
3 cloves garlic, chopped
1 Tbs powdered ginger
2 tsp salt
¾ tsp crushed red pepper flakes
1 Tbs sugar
1 tsp coriander
½ tsp powdered clove

3 lbs. beef (page 23)

½ cup oil
1 can tomato paste

1 can beef bouillon

*Serve with . . .
oatmeal-raisin bread
(American)
or
barley casserole
(Middle Eastern)
carrots with nutmeg
and honey (Flemish)
spinach salad with
orange and bacon
(American)
Wine suggestions:
red Bordeaux,
domestic claret*

BEEF WITH GINGER (*Burmese*)

Preparation . . .

1. Assemble and prepare all ingredients.
2. In container of electric blender, combine the first eight ingredients and blend for 20 seconds at low speed.

3. In onion-spice mixture, marinate meat for 4 hours. Stir several times if possible.
4. In 6-quart casserole, heat oil; add meat mixture and cook, stirring, to brown. Add tomato paste.

At this point you may stop and continue later.

Cooking . . .

5. Add bouillon to casserole, stir to blend ingredients, and bring to boil. Reduce heat and simmer, covered, for 2½ hours, or until meat is tender. More tomato paste and bouillon may be added if necessary.

If desired, 1 generous Tbs chopped ginger root may be added with tomato paste.

A *Malayan variation* omits tomato paste and bouillon, substituting ¼ cup lemon juice, 3 Tbs plum jam, and grated rind of one lemon, all thoroughly blended in 1 cup water.

BEEF WITH PAPRIKA (GOULASH) (*Hungarian*)

Serves 6
Doubles
Refrigerates
Freezes

TOTAL TIME:
about 3 hours
(30 minutes preparation,
2½ hours cooking)

You will need . . .

3 Tbs bacon fat (3 slices, rendered)
3 large onions, sliced thin
3 lbs. beef (page 23)
1 tsp salt
1 tsp sugar
2 Tbs paprika
2 cans tomato paste
1 tsp caraway seed

1 cup red Burgundy
Bouillon

1-lb. can small whole potatoes (optional)
2 Tbs paprika
2 Tbs melted butter
2 Tbs water

Serve with . . .
barley (Middle Eastern)
salad with dressing
sponge pudding (American)
Wine suggestions:
red Bordeaux,
domestic Burgundy

BEEF WITH PAPRIKA (GOULASH) (*Hungarian*)

Preparation . . .

1. Assemble and prepare all ingredients.
2. In 6-quart casserole, heat fat; cook onion until translucent. Add meat and brown, stirring to braise evenly. Season with salt, sugar, paprika. Add tomato paste and caraway seed.

    At this point you may stop and continue later.

Cooking . . .

3. Add wine first and then bouillon to cover. Bring casserole rapidly to boil; reduce heat and simmer, covered, for 2½ hours, or until meat is tender. More wine may be added if necessary.
4. If desired, potatoes may be added and heated through. Before serving, mix additional paprika with butter and water and stir into casserole. If desired, garnish with reserved bacon, crumbled.

    Variation: ½ lb. mushrooms, sliced and sautéed in 2 Tbs butter, may be used instead of potato.

GROUND BEEF WITH MUSHROOMS AND SOUR CREAM
(*Russian*)

Serves 6
Doubles
Refrigerates
Freezes

TOTAL TIME:
about 1 hour
(*30 minutes preparation,
30 minutes cooking*)

A quick and easy stroganov, as tasty as its elegant cousin made with tenderloin.

*Serve with . . .
bulgur or barley
(Middle Eastern)
salad with dressing
jellied sherry (Spanish)
Wine suggestions:
red Côtes du Rhone,
domestic Burgundy*

You will need . . .

4 Tbs butter
2 or 3 onions, minced
2 lbs. ground round
2 cloves garlic, sliced lengthwise

4 Tbs flour
¾ tsp salt
¼ tsp white pepper
1 lb. mushrooms, sliced

1 can cream of mushroom soup

1 cup sour cream

GROUND BEEF WITH MUSHROOMS AND SOUR CREAM
(*Russian*)

Preparation . . .

1. Assemble and prepare all ingredients.
2. In 6-quart casserole, melt butter and cook onion until translucent. Add meat and garlic and cook, stirring, until lightly browned.

Cooking . . .

3. Stir in flour and salt and pepper. Add mushrooms, cover and cook for 5 minutes.

4. Stir in soup and simmer, covered, for 10 minutes.

   At this point you may stop and continue later.

5. Add sour cream to simmering casserole, stirring; reduce heat and warm through—do not cook further. Before serving, remove garlic bits.

GROUND BEEF WITH OLIVES AND RICE (*Middle Eastern*)

Serves 6
Doubles
Refrigerates
Freezes

TOTAL TIME:
about 1¼ hours
(45 minutes preparation,
30 minutes cooking)

You will need . . .

1½ lbs. ground round
Olive oil

½ cup green pepper, chopped
½ cup onion, chopped
1 clove garlic, chopped

¾ cup pitted ripe (black) olives, halved
1½ cups raw natural rice

3 cups chicken broth
1 can tomato paste
1½ tsp salt
¼ tsp pepper

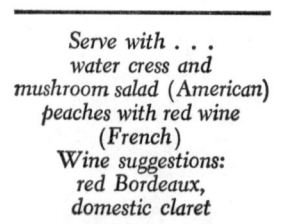

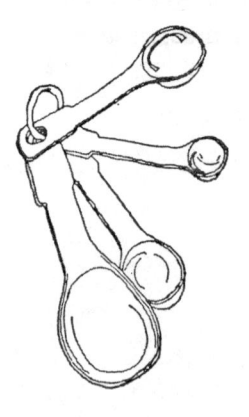

Serve with . . .
water cress and mushroom salad (American)
peaches with red wine (French)
Wine suggestions:
red Bordeaux,
domestic claret

GROUND BEEF WITH OLIVES AND RICE (*Middle Eastern*)

Preparation . . .

1. Assemble and prepare all ingredients.
2. In 6-quart casserole, brown meat (a little olive oil may be used if necessary). Remove.
3. In remaining fat (add additional oil if necessary), cook pepper, onion, and garlic until translucent.
4. Return meat to casserole; add olives and rice.

   At this point you may stop and continue later.

Cooking . . .

5. In saucepan, combine broth, tomato paste, and seasonings; bring to a boil and pour over casserole. Bake, covered, at 350° for 25 minutes, or until rice is tender and liquid is absorbed.

BEEF WITH ONIONS (*Greek*)

Serves 6
Doubles
Refrigerates
Freezes

TOTAL TIME:
about 3 hours
(*30 minutes preparation,
2½ hours cooking*)

You will need . . .

2 Tbs olive oil
2 Tbs butter
3 lbs. beef (page 23)
3 Tbs olive oil
18 small onions, peeled

2 cups whole canned Italian tomatoes
2 Tbs tomato paste
1 tsp salt
¼ tsp pepper
1 tsp sugar
2 cloves garlic, chopped
1 2″ piece stick cinnamon
6 whole cloves
2 bay leaves, broken
½ cup dry red wine

---
*Serve with . . .
barley casserole
(Middle Eastern)
spinach salad with
orange and bacon
(American)
Wine suggestions:
rosé d'Anjou,
domestic Burgundy*

BEEF WITH ONIONS (*Greek*)

Preparation . . .

1. Assemble and prepare all ingredients.
2. In 6-quart casserole, heat oil and butter; add meat and brown.
3. Add extra oil, then onions, and cook until onions are well-coated and slightly browned.

   At this point you may stop and continue later.

Cooking . . .

4. Combine these ten ingredients, pour over contents of casserole, and bring to boil; reduce heat and simmer, covered, for 2½ hours, or until meat is tender. More wine may be added if necessary.

BEEF WITH SAUERKRAUT (*Polish*)

*Serves 6 generously
Doubles
Refrigerates*

TOTAL TIME:
*about 2½ hours
(45 minutes preparation,
1¾ hours cooking)*

You will need . . .

5 strips thick-sliced bacon,
diced
2 onions, chopped

1 Tbs flour

2 lbs. beef (page 23)
¼ lb. garlic sausage, chopped
1 2-lb. can sauerkraut
¼ lb. mushrooms, sliced

2 Tbs butter
2 Tbs flour
1 cup beef bouillon
1 tsp salt
½ tsp pepper
2 Tbs sugar
3 Tbs parsley flakes

1 cup Madeira or sherry

*Serve with . . .
bread* en casserole,
*Variation II (American)
gingerbread (American)
Wine suggestions:
red Bordeaux,
domestic claret*

BEEF WITH SAUERKRAUT (*Polish*)

Preparation . . .

1. Assemble and prepare all ingredients.
2. In 6-quart casserole, cook bacon and onion until onions are translucent.
3. Add flour and continue to cook, stirring.
4. Add beef and brown slightly.
5. Add sausage, then sauerkraut and mushrooms; stir to blend ingredients. Simmer, covered, for 20 minutes.

   At this point you may stop and continue later.

6. In saucepan, melt butter and add flour, stirring; brown well. Add bouillon and cook, stirring, until sauce thickens. Add seasonings. Stir sauce into casserole.

Cooking . . .

7. Bake, covered, at 300° for 1½ hours.
8. Stir in wine and cook 15 minutes longer. If desired, garnish with reserved bacon.

BEEF WITH TAPIOCA (*American*)

Serves 6 generously
Doubles
Refrigerates
Freezes

TOTAL TIME:
5½ hours
(30 minutes preparation,
5 hours cooking)

You will need . . .

3 lbs. beef (page 23)
2 cups celery, chopped
6 large carrots, sliced
12 small onions, peeled
6 Tbs pearl tapioca
1 tsp salt
¼ tsp pepper
2 tsp sugar
1 tsp ground allspice
(optional)
2 Tbs parsley flakes
1 bay leaf, broken
1 2-lb. can whole Italian
tomatoes

Serve with . . .
bread en casserole,
Variation II (American)
salad with dressing
grapes with sour cream
(American)
Wine suggestions:
domestic or imported
red Burgundy

BEEF WITH TAPIOCA (*American*)

Preparation . . .

1. Assemble and prepare all ingredients.
   In 6-quart casserole, combine ingredients, stirring to mix all thoroughly.

At this point you may stop and continue later.

Cooking . . .

2. Bake, covered, at 250° for 5 hours, or until meat is tender. More tomatoes may be added if necessary.

BEEF WITH VEGETABLES (*American*)

Serves 6
Doubles
Refrigerates
Freezes

TOTAL TIME:
about 3 hours
(*45 minutes preparation,
2¼ hours cooking*)

You will need . . .

3 Tbs bacon fat (3 slices, rendered)
3 lbs. beef (page 23)
1 Tbs sugar

1 cup dry red wine
1 bay leaf, broken
6 whole cloves
2 cloves garlic, minced
3 Tbs parsley flakes
¼ tsp thyme
¼ tsp marjoram
1 tsp salt
¼ tsp pepper
2 cups beef bouillon

3 carrots, sliced
12 small white onions
12 mushrooms, quartered
3 small turnips, diced (optional)

1 box frozen peas, thawed

Serve with . . .
bread en casserole,
Variation I (*American*)
salad with dressing
gingerbread (*American*)
Wine suggestions:
red Burgundy,
domestic claret

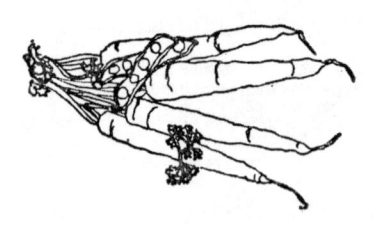

BEEF WITH VEGETABLES (*American*)

Preparation . . .

1. Assemble and prepare all ingredients.
2. In 6-quart casserole, heat fat; add meat and brown, stirring to braise evenly. Add sugar and continue cooking until meat is very dark.
3. In saucepan, combine these ten ingredients.

Cooking . . .

4. Bring contents of saucepan to boil, pour over meat, and bring casserole to boil: reduce heat and simmer, covered, for 30 minutes.

    At this point you may stop and continue later.

5. Add carrots, onions, mushrooms, and turnips. Continue cooking for 1½ hours, or until meat is tender.

6. Add peas and cook for 10 minutes longer. If desired, garnish with reserved bacon, crumbled.

BEEF WITH WHITE WINE AND SOUR CREAM
(*Hungarian*)

Serves 6
Doubles
Refrigerates
Freezes

TOTAL TIME:
about 3 hours
(*30 minutes preparation,*
2½ hours cooking)

You will need . . .

¼ lb. thick-sliced bacon, diced

6 onions, chopped
2 cloves garlic, chopped

3 lbs. beef (page 23)

1 tsp salt
¼ tsp pepper
1 tsp sugar
¾ tsp marjoram
1 cup dry white wine

1 pint sour cream

Serve with . . .
rice
vegetable casserole
(Hungarian)
Wine suggestions:
rosé d'Anjou,
domestic Burgundy

BEEF WITH WHITE WINE AND SOUR CREAM
(*Hungarian*)

Preparation . . .

1. Assemble and prepare all ingredients.
2. In 6-quart casserole, render bacon until crisp; remove to absorbent paper.
3. In remaining fat, cook onions and garlic until translucent.
4. Add meat and brown; stir to braise evenly.

At this point you may stop and continue later.

Cooking . . .

5. Add seasonings and wine. Bring to boil; reduce heat and simmer, covered, for 2¼ hours, or until meat is tender.

6. Stir in sour cream and simmer gently over lowest possible heat for 15 minutes; do not allow to boil. If desired, garnish with reserved bacon.

Casseroles made with Lamb

Lamb lends itself well to cooking *en casserole* for its flavor complements and is complemented by the ingredients accompanying it: hearty spices, fruit, and vegetables (especially eggplant). Lamb and curry are particularly felicitous together. The side dishes served with curried lamb—mango chutney, chopped sweet pickle, raisins, chopped egg, chopped scallions, pineapple tid-bits, shredded coconut, peanuts, thin-sliced banana, etc.—make a festive dining table. I include recipes for three lamb curries, each different from the others, in which the suggested amounts of curry powder yield a mild-spicy dish; timid souls may want to use less, adventurous ones will perhaps add more.

Lamb sold in supermarkets as "stewing lamb" is entirely adequate for the following recipes; it often tends to be fatty—and for this reason you may want to make the dish a day in advance, so that fat may be discarded from the refrigerated casserole. Ideal for casserole cookery is boned leg of lamb, cut into bite-size 1½" cubes; this is, however, a much more expensive cut of meat. Both varieties are flavorful, the leg being perhaps somewhat more delicate.

Recipes for the suggested side dishes given with each main dish may be found elsewhere in the book.

LAMB WITH APRICOTS (*Middle Eastern*)

Serves 6
Doubles
Refrigerates

TOTAL TIME:
about 2½ hours
(30 minutes preparation,
2 hours cooking)

You will need . . .

3 Tbs butter
3 lbs. lamb (page 57)

2 onions, chopped
1 tsp salt
¼ tsp pepper
1 tsp sugar
½ tsp paprika
1 tsp curry powder
¾ tsp ground cumin
¼ tsp ground allspice
¼ tsp ground cinnamon
2 bay leaves, broken

Boiling water

18 dried apricots, halved

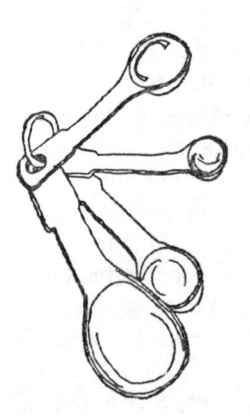

Serve with . . .
condiments for curries
rice,
salad with dressing
Wine suggestions:
red Bordeaux,
domestic claret

LAMB WITH APRICOTS (*Middle Eastern*)

Preparation . . .

1. Assemble and prepare all ingredients.
2. In 6-quart casserole, melt butter and brown lamb.
3. Add onion and the nine seasonings and cook until onion is translucent.

Cooking . . .

4. Add boiling water just to cover. Bake, covered, at 325° for 1¼ hours.

    At this point you may stop and continue later.

5. Add apricots and continue to bake, covered, for 45 minutes.

    If desired, casserole may be garnished with 3 Tbs chopped pimento and/or chopped fresh parsley.

LAMB WITH CUMIN AND SHERRY (*Spanish*)

Serves 6
Doubles
Refrigerates
Freezes

TOTAL TIME:
about 5½ hours
(30 minutes preparation,
4 hours marinating, 1 hour
cooking)

You will need . . .

3 lbs. lamb (page 57)
Dry sherry
Water

1 tsp salt
½ tsp pepper
2 tsp ground cumin

4 Tbs olive oil
3 cloves garlic, split

2 onions, chopped
2 Tbs flour
1 tsp ground cumin

1 cup sherry, boiling

Serve with . . .
brown rice with currants
and scallions (American)
salad with dressing
pears with red wine (French)
Wine suggestions:
domestic or imported
vin rosé

LAMB WITH CUMIN AND SHERRY (*Spanish*)

Preparation . . .

1. Assemble and prepare all ingredients.
   In equal parts sherry and water to cover, marinate lamb for 4 hours.

2. Drain and dry lamb; sprinkle with salt, pepper, and cumin. Discard marinade.

3. In 6-quart casserole, heat oil and cook garlic until oil is flavored, about 8 minutes. Remove garlic and reserve. Brown lamb in oil.

4. Add onions. Combine flour and cumin and add to meat mixture, stirring. Put reserved garlic through press, add, and stir well.

At this point you may stop and continue later.

Cooking . . .

5. Add sherry to casserole and simmer, covered, for 1 hour, or until meat is tender.

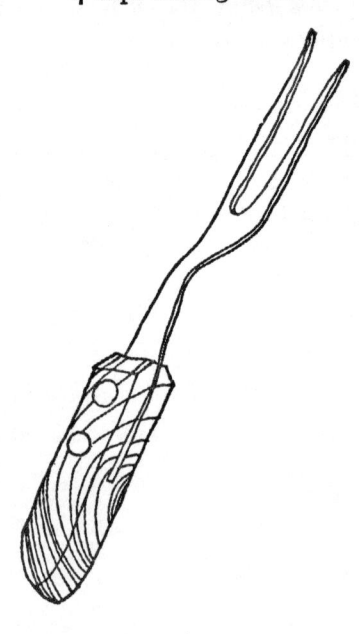

LAMB WITH CURRY AND LENTILS (*Indian*)

*Serves 6 generously
Doubles
Refrigerates
Freezes*

TOTAL TIME:
*about 4 hours
(30 minutes preparation,
2 hours marinating, 1½
hours cooking)*

You will need . . .

3 medium onions, chopped
2 cloves garlic, chopped
2 Tbs curry powder
1½ tsp salt
2 tsp sugar
½ cup yoghurt

3 lbs. lamb (page 57)

2 cups lentils
Boiling water

4 Tbs oil

4 cups boiling water

*Serve with . . .
spinach salad (French)
and cheese of your choice
dried fruit compote
Wine suggestions:
red Burgundy,
domestic rosé*

LAMB WITH CURRY AND LENTILS (*Indian*)

Preparation . . .

1. Assemble and prepare all ingredients.
2. In container of electric blender, combine the first six ingredients and blend for 20 seconds at low speed.
3. Toss lamb with onion-spice mixture and marinate for 2 hours.
4. Wash lentils; cover with boiling water, bring to second boil, and drain; discard water.

At this point you may stop and continue later.

Cooking . . .

5. In 6-quart casserole, heat oil; add lamb and marinade; simmer, covered, for 1 hour. Stir occasionally.
6. Add reserved lentils to casserole and then water, stirring. Simmer, covered, for 30 minutes, or until meat is tender and liquid is absorbed.

LAMB WITH CURRY—MAISON (*Indian*)

Serves 6
Doubles
Refrigerates
Freezes

TOTAL TIME:
about 2¼ hours
(45 minutes preparation,
1½ hours cooking)

You will need . . .

3 onions, chopped
4 Tbs butter
3 lbs. lamb (page 57)
Flour
Salt
Pepper
1 Tbs curry powder

4 cups beef bouillon
1½ tsp salt
1 bay leaf, broken
1 clove garlic, minced
½ tsp thyme
½ tsp marjoram
½ tsp dry mustard
½ tsp powdered ginger
½ tsp ground allspice
4 tsp brown sugar
1 can tomato paste

1 apple, peeled, cored, and cubed
1 Tbs cornstarch
¼ cup light cream

Serve with . . .
condiments for lamb curries
rice
cucumbers with yoghurt
and fresh herbs
(Middle Eastern)
Wine suggestions:
red Bordeaux,
domestic claret

LAMB WITH CURRY—MAISON (*Indian*)

Preparation . . .

1. Assemble and prepare all ingredients.
2. In 6-quart casserole, cook onions in butter until translucent.
3. Dredge lamb in seasoned flour and add to casserole. Sprinkle curry powder over all.

4. In separate saucepan, combine these eleven ingredients.

   At this point you may stop and continue later.

Cooking . . .

5. Bring liquid mixture to boil and pour over contents of casserole; cook, covered, at 350° for 1½ hours, or until meat is tender.

6. Just before serving, stir in apple; mix cornstarch with cream and add, stirring until sauce thickens slightly.

LAMB WITH CURRY AND TOMATOES (*Arabian*)

Serves 6
Doubles
Refrigerates
Freezes

TOTAL TIME:
about 2½ hours
(50 minutes preparation,
1½ hours cooking)

You will need . . .

4 Tbs butter
3 onions, chopped
2 cloves garlic, minced
2 Tbs curry powder
1 tsp salt
1 tsp sugar
½ tsp cayenne
1 tsp ground allspice
1 2-lb. can Italian tomatoes
1 1-lb. can tomato purée

3 lbs. lamb (page 57)

Serve with . . .
rice
cucumbers with oranges
and sour cream
(Middle Eastern)
Wine suggestions:
domestic or imported
vin rosé

LAMB WITH CURRY AND TOMATOES (*Arabian*)

Preparation . . .

1. Assemble and prepare all ingredients.
2. In 6-quart casserole, melt butter and cook onion until translucent. Add garlic, curry powder, and seasonings. Add tomatoes and tomato purée, stirring. Simmer, covered, for 30 minutes, stirring occasionally.

At this point you may stop and continue later.

Cooking . . .

3. Add lamb and simmer, covered, for 1½ hours, or until meat is tender. More tomato purée may be added if necessary.

LAMB WITH EGGPLANT (*Middle Eastern*)

*Serves 6
Doubles
Refrigerates
Freezes*

TOTAL TIME:
*about 2¼ hours
(45 minutes preparation,
1½ hours cooking)*

You will need . . .

2 Tbs oil
3 lbs. lamb (page 57)
6 medium onions, chopped

1 large eggplant, cubed
1 tsp paprika
1 tsp ground allspice
1 tsp salt
½ tsp pepper
1 tsp sugar

1 1-lb. can Italian tomatoes
1 cup dry red wine

*Serve with . . .
bulgur (Middle Eastern)
cucumber with yoghurt
and herbs (Middle Eastern)
or
peaches with curry
(Middle Eastern)
Wine suggestions:
red Bordeaux,
domestic claret*

LAMB WITH EGGPLANT (*Middle Eastern*)

Preparation . . .

1. Assemble and prepare all ingredients.
2. In 6-quart casserole, heat oil; brown lamb. Add onions and cook until translucent.

3. Add eggplant and seasonings.

At this point you may stop and continue later.

Cooking . . .

4. Add tomatoes and wine. Bake, covered, at 350° for 1½ hours, or until lamb is tender. A little water may be added if needed; the dish should be moist but not liquid.

GROUND LAMB WITH EGGPLANT (*Rumanian*)

Serves 6
Doubles
Refrigerates

TOTAL TIME:
about 2¼ hours
(1 hour preparation,
1¼ hours cooking)

You will need . . .

1 large eggplant, peeled and cut in ½" slices
Salt
1 medium onion, chopped
2 Tbs butter
2 lbs. ground lamb

Flour

3 or 4 ripe tomatoes, sliced

1 cup yoghurt
4 egg yolks
½ cup flour

Serve with . . .
bulgur (Middle Eastern)
cucumbers with oranges
and green pepper
(Middle Eastern)
and feta or goat cheese
(Greek)
Wine suggestions:
domestic or imported
vin rosé

GROUND LAMB WITH EGGPLANT (*Rumanian*)

Preparation . . .

1. Assemble and prepare all ingredients.
2. Salt each side of eggplant slices; let stand 1 hour. Meanwhile, in 6-quart casserole, cook onion in butter until translucent. Add lamb and brown slightly; remove. Pour off excess fat; reserve.

3. Dredge eggplant in flour and brown in fat remaining in casserole; reserved fat may be added, if needed.

   At this point you may stop and continue later.

Cooking . . .

4. In casserole, arrange alternate layers of lamb and eggplant. Top with tomatoes. Bake, covered, at 350° for 1 hour.

   At this point dish may be refrigerated.

   Mix thoroughly yoghurt, egg yolks, and flour; pour over casserole. Bake, uncovered, at 350° for 15 minutes, or until sauce browns on top.

LAMBCHOPS WITH EGGPLANT (*Italian*)

Serves 6
Doubles
Refrigerates
Freezes

TOTAL TIME:
about 2 hours
(*45 minutes preparation,*
1¼ hours cooking)

You will need . . .

½ cup olive oil
1 onion, chopped
1 clove garlic, chopped
6 large shoulder lamb chops

1 lb. fresh tomatoes, sliced
Salt
Pepper
Dried basil
Dried oregano
1 large eggplant, cut in 1" cubes
3 green peppers, chopped
1 cup natural raw rice
1 1-lb. can tomato purée
1 tsp sugar
1 tsp ground allspice

Serve with . . .
salad with dressing
and Italian cheese of
your choice
Wine suggestions:
domestic or imported
red chianti

LAMBCHOPS WITH EGGPLANT (*Italian*)

Preparation . . .

1. Assemble and prepare all ingredients.
2. In 6-quart casserole, heat oil; add onion and garlic and cook until translucent; remove. Add chops and brown; remove. Grease sides of casserole; pour off remaining oil and reserve.
3. On bottom of casserole, arrange layer of ½ the tomatoes; season with salt, pepper, basil, and oregano. Around edge of casserole, stand chops up with heart end down and bone side toward the center. Add ½ the eggplant, filling in between the chops to help them stand. Add ½ the pepper. Repeat with remaining tomatoes, seasonings, eggplant, and pepper. Add rice in an even layer. Combine purée with sugar and allspice and pour over all. Sprinkle with 3 Tbs reserved oil. Cover tightly; if chop bones prevent using casserole lid, heavy foil, carefully arranged to stop steam escaping, will do.

At this point you may stop and continue later.

Cooking . . .

4. Bake, covered, at 350° for 1¼ hours, or until rice is tender.

LAMB WITH FRUIT AND RICE (*Middle Eastern*)

Serves 6
Doubles
Refrigerates

TOTAL TIME:
about 4 hours
(30 minutes preparation,
2 hours fruit soaking,
1½ hours cooking)

You will need . . .

1 11-oz. package dried mixed fruit
Water

3 Tbs oil
3 lbs. lamb (page 57)

2 cloves garlic, minced
½ cup sugar
1 tsp cinnamon or ground allspice
1 tsp poultry seasoning
⅓ cup tarragon vinegar
1½ tsp salt
½ tsp pepper
Boiling water

1 cup natural raw rice

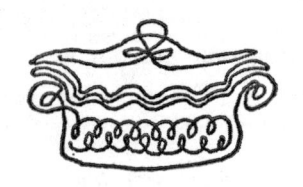

Serve with . . .
braised fennel with sherry
(French)
grapes with sour cream
(American)
Wine suggestions:
red Bordeaux,
domestic claret

LAMB WITH FRUIT AND RICE (*Middle Eastern*)

Preparation . . .

1. Assemble and prepare all ingredients.
2. Cover fruit with water and soak for 2 hours.
3. In 6-quart casserole, heat oil; brown lamb.

Cooking . . .

4. Add these seven ingredients to meat, together with boiling water to cover. Cook, covered, at 350° for 1 hour.

At this point you may stop and continue later.

5. To casserole, add rice and drained fruit; reserve fruit water. Continue cooking, covered, for ½ hour, or until lamb and rice are tender and liquid is absorbed. Reserved fruit water may be added as necessary.

LAMB WITH PAPRIKA (*Hungarian*)

Serves 6
Doubles
Refrigerates

TOTAL TIME:
about 2¾ hours
(45 minutes preparation,
2 hours cooking)

You will need . . .

3 Tbs bacon fat (3 slices, rendered)
3 lbs. lamb (page 57)

3 onions, chopped
1 clove garlic, minced
1 tsp salt
¼ tsp pepper
1 tsp sugar
1½ or 2 tsp paprika

1 1-lb. can tomato purée

1 cup sour cream

Serve with . . .
rice,
vegetable casserole
(Hungarian)
dried fruit compote
Wine suggestions:
domestic or imported
red Burgundy

LAMB WITH PAPRIKA (*Hungarian*)

Preparation . . .

1. Assemble and prepare all ingredients.
2. In 6-quart casserole, melt bacon fat and brown lamb. Remove and drain on absorbent paper. Pour off excess fat and return lamb to casserole.
3. To casserole, add onion, garlic, and seasonings.

At this point you may stop and continue later.

Cooking . . .

4. Add tomato purée and bring to boil; reduce heat and simmer, covered, stirring occasionally, for 1¾ hours, or until lamb is tender. More purée may be added if needed.
5. Add sour cream, stirring gently to blend; continue to cook over lowest possible heat for 15 minutes. Do not allow to boil. If desired, garnish with reserved bacon, crumbled.

LAMB WITH PARSLEY AND LENTILS (*Syrian*)

Serves 6
Doubles
Refrigerates
Freezes

TOTAL TIME:
about 2½ hours
(1 hour preparation,
1½ hours cooking)

You will need . . .

2 Tbs butter
4 Tbs oil
3 lbs. lamb (page 57)

4 bunches fresh parsley, chopped (without stems)
12 scallions, chopped (with as much green as possible)

1½ tsp salt
1 tsp sugar
½ tsp pepper
1 tsp ground allspice
1½ cups lentils, washed
Grated rind of 2 lemons

2 cups beef bouillon
1 cup dry red wine
Juice of 2 lemons

Serve with . . .
cucumbers with yoghurt
and fresh herbs
(Middle Eastern)
pears with curry
(Middle Eastern)
Wine suggestions:
domestic or imported
red Burgundy

LAMB WITH PARSLEY AND LENTILS (*Syrian*)

Preparation . . .

1. Assemble and prepare all ingredients.
2. In 6-quart casserole, heat butter and oil; brown lamb. Remove.
3. In remaining fat, cook parsley and scallions until parsley is dark green and scallions are translucent.
4. To casserole, add reserved meat, seasonings, lentils, and lemon rind.

At this point you may stop and continue later.

Cooking . . .

5. Combine liquids and add to casserole. Bring to boil; reduce heat and simmer, covered, for 1½ hours, or until lamb and lentils are tender and liquid is absorbed. More liquid (bouillon or water) may be added if necessary.

LAMB WITH RAISINS AND SPICES (*North African*)

*Serves 6
Doubles
Refrigerates*

TOTAL TIME:
*about 2½ hours
(45 minutes preparation,
1¾ hours cooking)*

You will need . . .

2 Tbs oil
3 lbs. lamb (page 57)
2 onions, minced
2 cloves garlic, minced
3 Tbs flour

1 cup white raisins
½ tsp saffron
¾ tsp ground cardamon
¼ tsp ground ginger
1½ tsp ground cinnamon
1½ tsp salt
¾ tsp pepper
2 cups beef bouillon

3 small yellow squash, peeled and cubed (or 1 box frozen)
Juice of 1 lemon

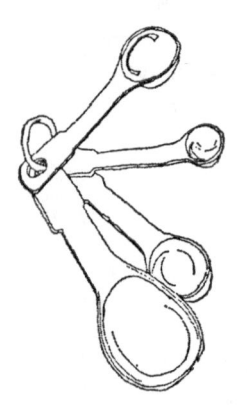

*Serve with . . .
bulgur (Middle Eastern)
spinach salad with
orange and bacon
(American)
Wine suggestions:
red Côtes du Rhone,
domestic vin rosé*

LAMB WITH RAISINS AND SPICES (*North African*)

Preparation . . .

1. Assemble and prepare all ingredients.
2. In 6-quart casserole, heat oil; brown lamb. Drain on absorbent paper. Discard fat, reserving 2 Tbs. In reserved fat, cook onion and garlic until onion is translucent. Add flour and cook until mixture is brown.

Cooking . . .

3. Return lamb to casserole, add raisins and seasonings; pour bouillon over all. Bring to boil; reduce heat and simmer, covered, for 1½ hours, or until lamb is tender.

At this point you may stop and continue later.

4. To simmering casserole, add squash and continue cooking for 15 minutes, or until squash is tender. Remove from heat and stir in lemon juice.

LAMB WITH SOUR CHERRIES (*American*)

Serves 6
Doubles
Refrigerates

TOTAL TIME:
about 2¾ hours
(1 hour preparation,
1¾ hours cooking)

You will need . . .

2 Tbs butter
3 lbs. lamb (page 57)
3 Tbs flour
6 scallions, chopped (with
as much green as possible)
2 1-lb. cans pitted sour cherries,
drained
½ cup white raisins
1 cup chicken broth
¾ cup port wine
1¼ tsp ground cardamon
1½ tsp salt
½ tsp pepper

1 2-lb. can kidney beans,
drained

Serve with . . .
oatmeal-raisin bread
(American)
Caesar salad (American)
or
muffins (American)
wilted lettuce salad
(American)
sponge pudding (American)
Wine suggestions:
domestic or imported
vin rosé

LAMB WITH SOUR CHERRIES (*American*)

Preparation . . .

1. Assemble and prepare all ingredients.

Cooking . . .

2. In 6-quart casserole, melt butter and brown lamb. Drain on absorbent paper. Discard fat. Return lamb to casserole and sprinkle with flour. Add scallions and the next seven ingredients; toss well. Bring to boil; reduce heat and simmer, covered, for 1½ hours, or until lamb is tender. More liquid may be added if necessary.

At this point you may stop and continue later.

3. To simmering casserole, add kidney beans and continue cooking for 15 minutes.

LAMB WITH VEGETABLES (*Irish*)

Serves 6
Doubles
Refrigerates
Freezes

TOTAL TIME:
about 2¾ hours
(1 hour preparation,
1¾ hours cooking)

"Irish stew," reliable, tasty, and filling. To brown lamb, fat cut from the meat is best, but bacon fat does nicely.

Serve with . . .
muffins (American)
salad with dressing
and cheese of your choice
Wine suggestions:
domestic or imported
red Burgundy

You will need . . .

3 Tbs melted lamb or bacon fat (3 slices, rendered)
3 lbs. lamb (page 57)

2 large onions, sliced
4 celery stalks with tops, chopped
2 cloves garlic, minced
1 Tbs (generous) brown sugar
1½ tsp salt
½ tsp pepper
2 potatoes, peeled and grated
2 cans clear chicken broth
Water

12 small onions, peeled
3 potatoes, peeled and cubed

1 package frozen peas, thawed

LAMB WITH VEGETABLES (*Irish*)

Preparation . . .

1. Assemble and prepare all ingredients.
2. In 6-quart casserole, melt fat and brown lamb.

Cooking . . .

3. Add onion, celery, garlic, seasonings, and shredded potato; then broth and water to cover. Bring to boil; reduce heat and simmer, covered, for 1 hour. (Liquid will thicken and grated potatoes disappear.)

At this point you may stop and continue later.

4. To contents of casserole, add onions and potatoes; cook for 30 minutes, or until lamb and potatoes are tender.

   Add peas and cook for 10 minutes. If desired, garnish with reserved bacon, crumbled.

GROUND LAMB WITH YOGHURT AND CURRY (*Indian*)

Serves 6
Doubles
Refrigerates

TOTAL TIME:
about 1 hour
(30 minutes preparation,
25 minutes cooking)

You will need . . .

3 Tbs butter
3 onions, chopped
2 lbs. ground lamb
1½ tsp salt
¾ tsp turmeric
1½ tsp ground coriander
¼ tsp red pepper flakes

1 cup yoghurt

1 package frozen peas, thawed

Serve with . . .
bulgur (Middle Eastern)
spinach salad (French)
Wine suggestions:
domestic or imported
red Burgundy

GROUND LAMB WITH YOGHURT AND CURRY (*Indian*)

Preparation . . .

1. Assemble and prepare all ingredients.
2. In 6-quart casserole, melt butter and cook onion until translucent. Add lamb and seasonings and brown over medium heat, stirring.

At this point you may stop and continue later.

Cooking . . .

3. Add yoghurt, stirring. Cook over low heat for 10 minutes.
4. Add peas and cook for 15 minutes longer. A little water may be added if needed.

Casseroles made with Pork

Perhaps Charles Lamb in his essay "Of Roast Pig" has forever won me over to pork *nature*—pork roast, broiled pork chops, and so forth—for I seem to have discovered few recipes for pork *en casserole* which excite my appetite sufficiently to want to share them. There are three pork dishes, however, which I find especially appealing: Pork with Apricots, Pork with Beer and Vegetables, and the classic Pork with Sauerkraut (*choucroute alsacienne*). The first dish is light; the latter two are hearty.

Recipes for the suggested side dishes given with each main dish may be found elsewhere in the book.

PORK WITH APRICOTS (*Italian*)

*Serves 6
Doubles
Refrigerates*

TOTAL TIME:
*about 2 hours
(30 minutes preparation,
1½ hours cooking)*

You will need . . .

2 lbs. shoulder of pork,
cut in bite-size pieces
3 onions, chopped
1 clove garlic, minced
1 tsp dried mint leaves
24 dried apricot halves
1 tsp dill weed, dried
1 tsp salt
¼ tsp pepper
1 tsp sugar

2 cups dry red wine

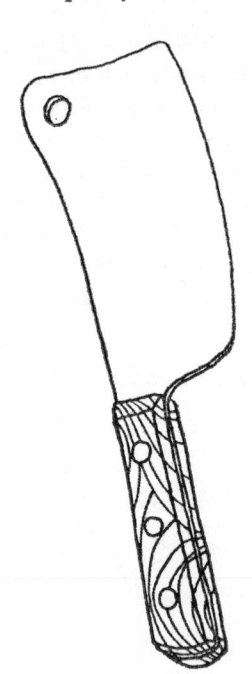

*Serve with . . .
rice with saffron and
tomatoes
spinach salad (French)
and cheese of your choice
Wine suggestions:
domestic or imported
vin rosé*

PORK WITH APRICOTS (*Italian*)

Preparation . . .

1. Assemble and prepare all ingredients.

   In 6-quart casserole, arrange pork, then onions and garlic, mint, apricots, dill, salt, pepper, and sugar.

   At this point you may stop and continue later.

Cooking . . .

2. Pour wine over all and cook, covered, at 350° for 1½ hours, or until pork is tender.

PORK WITH BEER AND VEGETABLES (*Flemish*)

*Serves 6
Doubles
Refrigerates
Freezes*

TOTAL TIME:
*about 2 hours
(30 minutes preparation,
1½ hours cooking)*

You will need . . .

2 Tbs bacon fat (3 slices, rendered)
2 lbs. shoulder of pork,
cut in bite-size pieces

1 tsp salt
½ tsp pepper
1 tsp sugar
1 tsp rosemary, crumbled
1 12-oz. can beer

6 onions, halved
6 carrots, sliced

3 Tbs flour
3 Tbs cold water

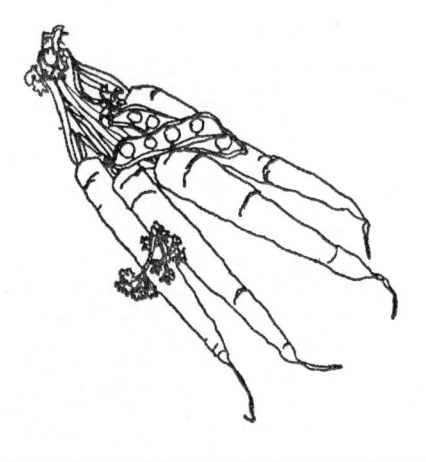

*Serve with . . .
bock beer bread (German)
water cress and mushroom
salad (American)
and cheese of your choice
Wine suggestions:
domestic or imported
red Burgundy*

PORK WITH BEER AND VEGETABLES (*Flemish*)

Preparation . . .

1. Assemble and prepare all ingredients.
2. In 6-quart casserole, melt bacon fat and brown meat.

Cooking . . .

3. Add seasonings, beer, and bring to boil; reduce heat and simmer, covered, for 45 minutes.

4. Add vegetables and continue cooking for 30 minutes, or until meat and vegetables are tender.

   At this point you may stop and continue later.

5. Combine flour and water, stirring to make a smooth paste. Add to casserole and cook, stirring, until sauce thickens. If desired, garnish with reserved bacon, crumbled.

PORK WITH SAUERKRAUT (*Alsatian*)

Serves 6
Doubles
Refrigerates

TOTAL TIME:
about 2¾ hours
(30 minutes preparation,
2¼ hours cooking)

You will need . . .

2 lbs. sauerkraut, rinsed and drained
½ lb. thick-sliced bacon, diced
6 porkchops
2 cloves garlic, split
2 bay leaves, broken
2 cups dry white wine

6 medium potatoes, peeled

6 *wurst* sausages

This recipe for choucroute alsacienne *comes from Strasbourg.*

Serve with . . .
gingerbread (American)
Wine suggestions:
red Bordeaux,
domestic claret

PORK WITH SAUERKRAUT (*Alsatian*)

Preparation . . .

1. Assemble and prepare all ingredients.
2. In 6-quart casserole, arrange even layer of ½ the sauerkraut. Add, in order, bacon, porkchops, and remaining sauerkraut. Distribute garlic sections and bay leaf. Pour wine over all.

Cooking . . .

3. Bring to boil; reduce heat, and simmer, covered, for 1 hour.

   At this point you may stop and continue later.

4. Add potatoes and continue cooking for 1 hour.
5. 15 minutes before serving, add sausages.

Casseroles made with Rabbit

Today the food fancier does not have to go abroad for a flavorful *civet de lapin*. Indeed, he never did have to do so, had he known that better butchers carry rabbit raised for eating and that rabbit is also available fully dressed and frozen. While rabbit tastes something like chicken, its flavor is individual and delicate and deserves to be enjoyed on its own merit. If you use fresh-killed rabbit, ask the butcher to dress and cut it into serving pieces. If you use the frozen variety, allow it to thaw completely and then dry it with absorbent paper before preparing the dish.

Recipes for the suggested side dishes given with each main dish may be found elsewhere in the book.

RABBIT WITH MUSHROOMS AND SOUR CREAM
(*Hungarian*)

Serves 6
Doubles
Refrigerates

TOTAL TIME:
about 2¼ hours
(*45 minutes preparation,*
1½ hours cooking)

You will need . . .

3 lbs. tender young rabbit,
cut into serving pieces
Flour
Salt
Pepper

4 strips thick-sliced bacon,
diced

3 onions, chopped
3 stalks celery, chopped
3 carrots, sliced thin
¼ tsp each: thyme
ground allspice
crushed peppercorn
1 bay leaf, broken
1 tsp sugar

1 1-lb. can tomato purée

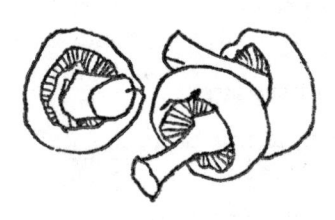

1 cup sour cream
½ lb. sliced mushrooms,
sautéed

Serve with . . .
bulgur (Middle Eastern)
braised endive (French)
pears with red wine
(French)
Wine suggestions:
domestic or imported
vin rosé

RABBIT WITH MUSHROOMS AND SOUR CREAM
(Hungarian)

Preparation . . .

1. Assemble and prepare all ingredients.
2. Dredge rabbit in seasoned flour.

3. In 6-quart casserole, render bacon until crisp; remove to absorbent paper and reserve. In remaining fat, brown rabbit pieces.
4. Add vegetables and seasonings.

Cooking . . .

5. Add purée, bring casserole to boil; reduce heat and simmer, covered, for 1½ hours, or until meat is tender.

   At this point you may stop and continue later.

   Also, at this point, dish may be refrigerated.
6. To simmering casserole, add sour cream and mushrooms, stirring to blend; cook over lowest possible heat for 15 minutes. Do not allow to boil. Garnish with reserved bacon.

RABBIT WITH ORANGE SAUCE (*French*)

*Serves 6
Doubles
Refrigerates
Freezes*

TOTAL TIME:
*about 2¼ hours
(45 minutes preparation,
1½ hours cooking)*

You will need . . .

3 lbs. tender young rabbit,
cut into serving pieces
Flour
Salt
Pepper

4 Tbs oil

1 large green pepper,
chopped
½ lb. mushrooms, sliced

2 cups orange juice
1 cup chicken broth
4 Tbs lemon juice
Grated rind of 2 oranges

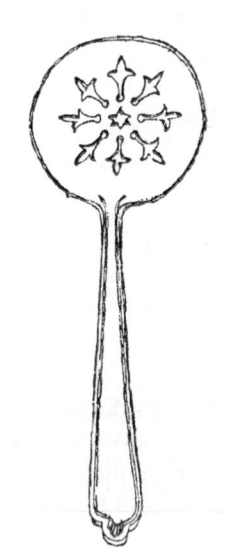

*Serve with . . .
gougère (French)
spinach salad (French)
individual chocolate mousse
(French)
Wine suggestions:
rosé d'Anjou,
domestic dry sauterne*

RABBIT WITH ORANGE SAUCE (*French*)

Preparation . . .

1. Assemble and prepare all ingredients.
2. Dredge rabbit in seasoned flour.//
3. In 6-quart casserole, heat oil; brown rabbit.
4. Add pepper and mushrooms and cook for 5 minutes.
5. Combine liquids and orange rind.

    At this point you may stop and continue later.

Cooking . . .

6. Pour orange juice mixture over all and bring to boil; reduce heat and simmer, covered, for 1½ hours, or until meat is tender.

RABBIT WITH RED WINE (*French*)

Serves 6
Doubles
Refrigerates
Freezes

TOTAL TIME:
about 2¼ hours
(45 minutes preparation,
1½ hours cooking)

You will need . . .

4 Tbs butter
3 lbs. tender young rabbit,
cut in bite-size pieces
2 onions, chopped

2 Tbs flour
1 tsp salt
½ tsp pepper
1 tsp sugar
½ tsp rosemary
1 cup water
2 cups red wine
Juice and grated rind of 1 lemon

½ square bitter chocolate, grated

Serve with . . .
bread en casserole
(French)
carrots with orange and
honey (Flemish)
spinach salad (French)
and French cheese of your
choice
Wine suggestions:
white Burgundy,
domestic Chablis

RABBIT WITH RED WINE (*French*)

Preparation . . .

1. Assemble and prepare all ingredients.
2. In 6-quart casserole, melt butter and brown rabbit. Add onions and cook until translucent.

   At this point you may stop and continue later.

Cooking . . .

3. Sprinkle flour over contents of casserole, stirring. Add seasonings. Combine water, and wine, lemon juice and rind, and pour over all. Bring casserole to boil; reduce heat and simmer, covered, for 1 hour.

4. Stir in chocolate and continue cooking for 30 minutes (chocolate gives rich color to sauce).

Casseroles made with Veal

Delicate and sweet-flavored, veal is ideal for "light" main dish casseroles, particularly appetizing for mild-weather meals. Veal enjoys the company of spices, vegetables, and is especially complimented by fruit flavors. For the following seven recipes, I use stewing veal as packaged by the supermarket; it is not necessary to pay the premium price of leg of veal, deboned. Before preparing the recipe, I look over the packaged veal, trimming it and cutting it into bite-size pieces.

Recipes for the suggested side dishes given with each main dish may be found elsewhere in the book.

VEAL WITH ORANGES (*Spanish*)

Serves 6
Doubles
Refrigerates

TOTAL TIME:
about 2 hours
(*30 minutes preparation,
1½ hours cooking*)

You will need . . .

3 Tbs butter
3 lbs. stewing veal, cut in bite-size pieces
1 tsp salt
½ tsp pepper
1 Tbs brown sugar

4 carrots, sliced
4 oranges, sliced paper-thin and seeded
2 cups chicken broth

⅔ cup sherry

Serve with . . .
bread en casserole (*French*)
wilted lettuce salad (*American*)
rice pudding (*Greek*)
Wine suggestions: Neuchâtel, domestic Chablis

VEAL WITH ORANGES (*Spanish*)

Preparation . . .

1. Assemble and prepare all ingredients.
2. In 6-quart casserole, melt butter and brown meat. Add seasonings.

Cooking . . .

3. Add carrots and oranges to casserole, pour broth over, and bring to boil; reduce heat and simmer, covered, for about 1¼ hours, or until meat and carrots are tender.

   At this point you may stop and continue later.

4. Add sherry and continue cooking for 15 minutes.

VEAL WITH ORIENTAL SPICES (Ceylonese)

Serves 6
Doubles
Refrigerates
Freezes

TOTAL TIME:
*about 2 hours
(30 minutes preparation,
1½ hours cooking)*

Serve with . . .
rice
salad with dressing
pears with curry
(Middle Eastern)
Wine suggestions:
white Burgundy,
domestic Chablis

You will need . . .

3 lbs. stewing veal,
cut in bite-size pieces
Flour
Salt
Pepper
4 Tbs oil

1 onion, chopped
3 cloves garlic, minced
1 tsp salt
1 tsp powdered ginger
1 tsp sugar
2 tsp ground coriander
1 tsp turmeric
½ tsp powdered cumin
1½ tsp ground nutmeg
2" piece cinnamon bark
2 tsp chili powder

¼ cup cider vinegar
2 cups water

VEAL WITH ORIENTAL SPICES (*Ceylonese*)

Preparation . . .

1. Assemble and prepare all ingredients.
2. Dredge meat in seasoned flour. In 6-quart casserole, heat oil; brown meat.
3. Add onion, garlic, and the nine seasonings.

At this point you may stop and continue later.

Cooking . . .

4. To casserole, add vinegar and water. Bring to boil; reduce heat and simmer, covered, for 1½ hours, or until veal is tender.

VEAL WITH PAPRIKA (*Austrian*)

Serves 6
Doubles

TOTAL TIME:
about 2¼ hours
(*30 minutes preparation,
1¾ hours cooking*)

You will need . . .

3 lbs. stewing veal,
cut in bite-size pieces
Flour
Salt
Pepper
¼ lb. butter
1 onion, chopped
2 or 3 tsp paprika (to taste)

1 1-lb. can tomato purée

1 cup sour cream

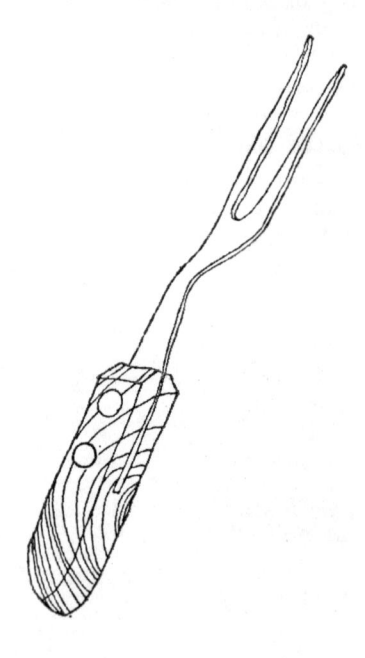

Serve with . . .
barley casserole
(Middle Eastern)
carrots with honey (Flemish)
peaches with red wine
(French)
Wine suggestions:
domestic or imported
Rhine wine

VEAL WITH PAPRIKA (*Austrian*)

Preparation . . .

1. Assemble and prepare all ingredients.
2. Dredge meat in seasoned flour. In 6-quart casserole, melt butter and brown meat; add onion and paprika and cook until onion is translucent. Stir often.

Cooking . . .

3. Add purée and bring to boil; reduce heat and simmer, covered, for 1½ hours, or until veal is tender.

    At this point you may stop and continue later.

    Also, at this point, dish may be refrigerated or frozen.

4. Add sour cream to simmering casserole and cook very gently for 15 minutes, stirring frequently. Do not allow to boil.

Variations:

1. add ½ cup chopped celery with sour cream
2. add ¼ lb. sliced sautéed mushrooms with sour cream
3. add 1 cup *very* thinly sliced carrots with tomato purée
4. substitute yoghurt for sour cream
5. garnish with toasted slivered almonds or sprinkle with poppy seed.

VEAL WITH PEARS (*Middle Eastern*)

Serves 6
Doubles
Refrigerates

TOTAL TIME:
about 2 hours
(30 minutes preparation,
1½ hours cooking)

You will need . . .

4 Tbs butter
3 lbs. stewing veal,
cut in bite-size pieces

2 onions, chopped
1 tsp salt
¼ tsp pepper
1 tsp sugar
½ tsp ground cinnamon
1 tsp dried mint flakes
½ cup water

6 firm pears cut in lengthwise eighths
Grated rind and juice of 1 lemon
2 Tbs brown sugar

Serve with . . .
barley casserole
(Middle Eastern)
salad with dressing
peaches with curry
(Middle Eastern)
Wine suggestions:
rosé d'Anjou,
domestic Chablis

VEAL WITH PEARS (*Middle Eastern*)

Preparation . . .

1. Assemble and prepare all ingredients.
2. In 6-quart casserole, melt butter and brown veal.

Cooking . . .

3. Add onions and cook until translucent. Add seasonings. Add water and bring to boil; reduce heat and simmer, covered, for 1 hour, or until veal is just tender. More water may be added if necessary.

    At this point you may stop and continue later.

4. To contents of simmering casserole add layer of pear slices. Sprinkle with lemon rind and juice and brown sugar. Continue to cook, covered, for 20 to 30 minutes, or until pears are tender.

    Six tart cooking apples, peeled, cored, and cut in lengthwise eighths, may be substituted for the pears.

    If fresh mint is available, omit dried mint flakes and garnish finished casserole with chopped mint leaves.

VEAL WITH SOUR CREAM AND MUSHROOMS (*Russian*)

Serves 6
Doubles
Refrigerates
Freezes

TOTAL TIME:
about 2½ hours
(30 minutes preparation,
1¾ hours cooking)

You will need . . .

3 Tbs butter
3 lbs. stewing veal, cut in thin slices and flattened with meat mallet
1 tsp salt
½ tsp pepper
1 tsp sugar
¾ tsp thyme

Juice and grated rind of 1 lemon
¾ cup consommé
½ lb. mushrooms, sliced

A *stroganov treatment for veal—very delicate in flavor.*

2 cups sour cream
Fresh dill, chopped (or dried)

Serve with . . .
barley casserole
(Middle Eastern)
salad with dressing
jellied sherry (Spanish)
Wine suggestions:
Moselle, domestic Chablis

VEAL WITH SOUR CREAM AND MUSHROOMS (*Russian*)

Preparation . . .

1. Assemble and prepare all ingredients.
2. In 6-quart casserole, melt butter and brown meat. Add seasonings.

Cooking . . .

3. Combine lemon juice, rind, and consommé, add to casserole, together with mushrooms, and bring to boil; reduce heat and simmer, covered, for 1½ hours, or until meat is tender.

   At this point you may stop and continue later.

4. Add sour cream, stirring to blend; cook over lowest possible heat for 15 minutes. Do not allow to boil. Just before serving, sprinkle with dill.

VEAL WITH VEGETABLES (*French*)

Serves 6
Doubles
Refrigerates
Freezes

TOTAL TIME:
about 1¾ hours
(30 minutes preparation,
1¼ hours cooking)

You will need . . .

3 lbs. stewing veal,
cut in bite-size pieces
¼ lb. bacon, cut in ½" strips
Water to cover

12 small onions, peeled
6 to 8 carrots, cut in ½" slices
½ lb. mushrooms, halved

"Blanquette de veau," *is a satisfying one-dish meal and light.*

4 Tbs flour
4 Tbs butter
2 cups stock from cooked veal
¼ cup cream
4 Tbs parsley, chopped
Juice and grated rind of 1 lemon
2 egg yolks, beaten

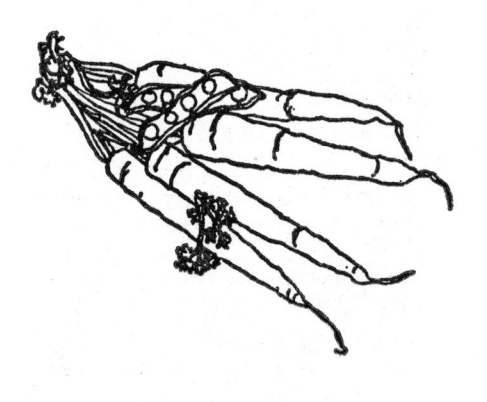

Serve with . . .
rice salad with dressing
and French cheese of your choice
individual chocolate mousse (French)
Wine suggestions:
Vouvray, domestic Chablis

VEAL WITH VEGETABLES (*French*)

Preparation . . .

1. Assemble and prepare all ingredients.

Cooking . . .

2. In kettle, boil veal and bacon vigorously for 45 minutes; skim.

3. Add vegetables to stewing meat and simmer, covered, for about 20 minutes, or until carrots are just tender.

   At this point you may stop and continue later.

4. In 6-quart casserole, melt butter and add flour, stirring; add veal stock, cream, parsley, lemon juice and rind, and egg yolks. Cook, stirring, until sauce thickens (about 10 minutes).

5. Drain veal and vegetables (reserve remaining stock for some other recipe); add to casserole, blending with sauce. Serve.

   Evaporated milk may be substituted for cream.

Casseroles made with Variety Meats

The following recipes are offered in belief that they are either a bit original or standard fare made more appealing by original treatment. Of the main ingredients—oxtail, beef tongue, sausages—only tripe needs introduction. When the idea of this book first occurred to me, I was asked if I intended including recipes made with tripe. It had, indeed, never occurred to me to omit them, and I had difficulty in narrowing down my choices to the two herewith presented.

In France it is said that tripe is enjoyed by two groups: the poor, because they can afford it; and gourmets, because they can appreciate it. Though many people eat liver and kidney quite happily, they are kept from discovering tripe because of cloudy prejudices against it. I once had a guest who, when told that tripe with carrots and onions was to be the main supper dish, blanched perceptibly. Later, when no vestige of the stew remained and the guest's complexion was far rosier, it was suggested that for next day I might make something else with tripe!

Today tripe is available completely cleaned and pot-ready. If your butcher has no fresh tripe, the chances are that he carries frozen tripe. In this case, allow it to thaw before starting the dish.

Recipes for the suggested side dishes given with each main dish may be found elsewhere in the book.

VEAL WITH SAUSAGE AND BEANS (*French*)

Serves 10
Doubles
Refrigerates
Freezes

TOTAL TIME:
about 5 hours
(1 hour preparation,
4 hours cooking)

Cassoulet, the Gallic relative of baked beans, requires two pots and one casserole—but is well worth the washing up! This is a simplified version; the native one often includes duck and lamb in addition to the meats listed here.

You will need . . .

1 lb. red beans
1 lb. pinto beans
Water to cover

2 large onions, chopped
1½ tsp salt
½ tsp pepper
2 tsp sugar
2 bay leaves, crushed
6 whole cloves
8 slices bacon, diced
1 lb. marrow bone

1 lb. sausage meat
2 lbs. veal, cut in bite-size pieces

4 cloves garlic, minced
1 Tbs tomato paste
2 onions, chopped
4 Tbs parsley, chopped
1 tsp rosemary
1 tsp thyme
2 cups dry white wine

Serve with . . .
braised endive (French)
or
ratatouille (French)
or
spinach salad (French)
with French cheese of your choice
dried fruit compote
Wine suggestions:
domestic or imported
dry sauterne

VEAL WITH SAUSAGE AND BEANS (*French*)

Preparation . . .

1. Assemble and prepare all ingredients.
2. Rinse beans and soak overnight.

Cooking . . .

3. In soup kettle, combine beans, bean water (add more water as necessary), seasonings, bacon and marrow bone. Bring to boil; reduce heat and simmer, covered, until beans are just tender (about 1½ hours).

4. Make marble-size balls of sausage meat. In large skillet, brown sausage; remove. Reserve 4 Tbs fat. Add veal to skillet and brown.
5. Add these seven ingredients to veal; simmer, covered, for 1 hour. Remove from heat and add sausage balls.

   At this point you may stop and continue later.

6. In 6-quart casserole, arrange alternate layers of bean and meat mixtures, including liquids from both. Bake, covered, at 350° for 1 hour; uncover and continue baking for 30 minutes.

   Though called for in no French recipe I have seen, I enjoy the zest the grated rind and juice of 1 lemon give. Add to the veal-sausage mixture when combining with the beans.

BAKED BEANS AND FRANKS (*American*)

Serves 10
Doubles
Refrigerates
Freezes

TOTAL TIME:
about 6½ hours
(*30 minutes preparation,
6 hours cooking*)

The home-cooked bean is only a nodding acquaintance of the canned variety; every advantage of quality, breeding, and good-taste is on the side of the bean you prepare yourself. This classic American dish is ideal for informal entertaining; for this reason the recipe is for ten servings.

You will need . . .

2 lbs. California or New York pea beans
Water to cover
1 tsp baking soda

1 lb. salt pork, cut in 1″ cubes
2 onions, chopped

1 cup blackstrap molasses
2 tsp dry mustard
4 tsp salt
½ tsp pepper
1 cup reserved bean water

20 frankfurters, broiled or pan-grilled

Serve with . . .
hot slaw (*American*)
seedless grapes with sour cream (*American*)
Wine suggestions:
domestic or imported vin rosé

BAKED BEANS AND FRANKS (*American*)

Preparation . . .

1. Assemble and prepare all ingredients.
2. Rinse beans and soak overnight. Next day, add water and soda and parboil for ten minutes. Drain, reserving water. Rinse beans with cold water.
3. On bottom of 6-quart casserole, arrange ½ of the salt pork and all the onion. Add beans and then remaining pork.
4. Combine molasses and seasonings with reserved water.

At this point you may stop and continue later.

Cooking . . .

5. Pour liquid to cover over contents of casserole; more reserved water may be added as needed. Bake, covered, at 300° for 6 hours, or until beans are tender.
6. Serve with frankfurters.

Maple syrup may be used instead of molasses (the flavor is more delicate). For extra zip, 2 Tbs Worcestershire sauce may be added to liquid. Bouillon or beer may be used instead of bean water.

OXTAIL WITH ONIONS (*French*)

Serves 6
Doubles
Refrigerates
Freezes

TOTAL TIME:
about 2¾ hours
(45 minutes preparation,
2 hours cooking)

You will need . . .

3 lbs. oxtail, disjointed
Flour
Salt
Pepper
6 Tbs bacon fat (6 slices, rendered)

1 cup celery, chopped
1 cup carrots, chopped
2 cloves garlic, minced

2 or 3 bay leaves
1 tsp thyme
4 Tbs parsley, chopped
1 tsp sugar
¾ tsp ground clove
1 2-lb. can whole Italian tomatoes
12 white onions, peeled
Bouillon
Dry red wine
1½ tsp salt
½ tsp pepper

1 lb. mushrooms, sliced

6 Tbs cognac

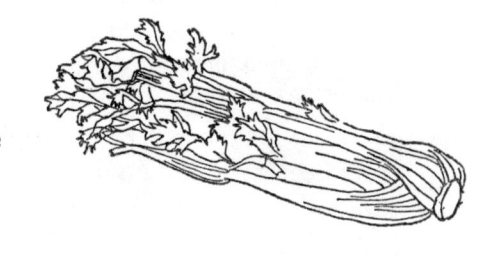

Serve with . . .
gougère (French)
or
bread en casserole
(French)
salad with dressing and
French cheese of your choice
peaches with red wine
(French)
Wine suggestions:
red Côtes du Rhone,
domestic claret

OXTAIL WITH ONIONS (*French*)

Preparation . . .

1. Assemble and prepare all ingredients.
2. Dredge oxtail in seasoned flour. In 6-quart casserole, heat fat and brown oxtail.
3. Add vegetables and garlic; continue to cook for 15 minutes, stirring.

Cooking . . .

4. Add seasonings, tomatoes, and onions; then equal parts bouillon and wine to cover (about 1½ cups each), sprinkle with salt and pepper. Bring to boil; reduce heat and simmer, covered, for 1½ to 2 hours, or until oxtail is tender.

At this point you may stop and continue later.

5. Add mushrooms to gently simmering casserole; cook 15 minutes.
6. Just before serving, heat cognac, ignite, and pour over casserole. If desired, garnish with reserved bacon, crumbled.

OXTAIL WITH RAISINS AND OLIVES (*American*)

Serves 6
Doubles
Refrigerates
Freezes

TOTAL TIME:
about 3¼ hours
(45 minutes preparation,
2½ hours cooking)

You will need . . .

3 lbs. oxtail, disjointed
¼ cup flour
Salt
Pepper
2 Tbs oil

½ tsp chili powder
2 tsp dry mustard
1 12-oz. can pineapple juice
Juice and grated rind 1 lemon
½ cup raisins
2 cups water

1 8-oz. can pitted ripe
(black) olives, halved
2 cups celery, chopped
2 green peppers, chopped

Serve with . . .
bread en casserole,
Variation IV
hot slaw (German)
pears with red wine
(French)
Wine suggestions:
domestic or imported
red Burgundy

OXTAIL WITH RAISINS AND OLIVES (*American*)

Preparation . . .

1. Assemble and prepare all ingredients.
2. Dredge oxtail in seasoned flour. In 6-quart casserole, heat oil; brown meat well and drain on absorbent paper. Discard fat.

Cooking . . .

3. Return oxtail to casserole. Add these seven ingredients. Bring to boil; reduce heat and simmer, covered, for 1½ to 2 hours, or until meat is just tender. Remove from heat. Cool; refrigerate.

   At this point stop; continue later.

4. Skim fat from cooled casserole. Allow to reach room temperature. Add olives, celery, and peppers. Bake, covered, at 375° for 45 minutes.

SAUSAGE WITH BEANS (*Mexican*)

*Serves 6
Doubles
Refrigerates
Freezes*

TOTAL TIME:
*about 2¼ hours
(45 minutes preparation,
1½ hours cooking)*

You will need . . .

1 lb. sausage meat
½ lb. Italian hot sausage meat
1 lb. ground round

2 2-lb. cans kidney beans, drained
1 1-lb. can whole Italian tomatoes
1 large onion, chopped
1 clove garlic, chopped
1 bay leaf
1 tsp salt
½ tsp sugar
½ tsp thyme

1 cup potatoes, diced
½ green pepper, chopped

*Serve with . . .
guacamole (Mexican)
salad with dressing
Wine suggestions:
red Bordeaux,
domestic claret*

SAUSAGE WITH BEANS (*Mexican*)

Preparation . . .

1. Assemble and prepare all ingredients.
2. In 6-quart casserole, cook meats for about 25 minutes, until well done; drain. Discard fat.

Cooking . . .

3. Combine meats with these eight ingredients. Simmer, covered, for 1 hour. Add more tomatoes, if needed.

At this point you may stop and continue later.

4. Add potato and pepper to simmering casserole; continue to cook, covered, for 20 minutes, or until potato is tender.

SAUSAGE WITH CABBAGE AND APPLES (*American*)

Serves 6
Doubles
Refrigerates

TOTAL TIME:
about 1½ hours
(45 minutes preparation,
45 minutes cooking)

You will need . . .

2 lbs. sausage meat, made into 12 patties

¼ cup cider vinegar
1 medium onion, minced
4 Tbs brown sugar

1 large cabbage, shredded
6 apples, peeled, thinly sliced
Salt
Pepper
Freshly grated nutmeg

Serve with . . .
gingerbread (American)
Wine suggestions:
domestic or imported
vin rosé

SAUSAGE WITH CABBAGE AND APPLES (*American*)

Preparation . . .

1. Assemble and prepare all ingredients.
2. In 6-quart casserole, cook sausage on both sides until slightly brown. Remove and reserve. Reserve ¼ cup fat.
3. Add these three ingredients to fat and cook briefly; pour off and reserve.
4. In casserole, arrange alternate layers of cabbage and apples; season each layer with sprinkling of salt, pepper, and nutmeg. Arrange sausage patties on top.

At this point you may stop and continue later.

Cooking . . .

5. Pour hot vinegar sauce over all. Bake, covered, at 375° for 45 minutes.

SAUSAGES WITH RATATOUILLE (*French*)

Serves 6
Doubles
Refrigerates

TOTAL TIME:
about 1¾ hours
(45 minutes preparation,
1 hour cooking)

Ratatouille (*see also under
"Vegetables," p. 262*) *is a
Provençal vegetable stew.
The addition of sausages
makes it an unusual main
dish.*

Serve with . . .
salad with dressing
and French cheese of your
choice
individual chocolate mousse
(French)
Wine suggestions:
red Bordeaux,
domestic claret

You will need . . .

½ cup olive oil
2 large onions, sliced
3 cloves garlic, minced
1 medium eggplant, cut in 1" cubes
2 green peppers, chopped
3 zucchini, cut in ½" slices

1 2-lb. can whole Italian tomatoes, drained (reserve liquid)
1 tsp salt
¼ tsp pepper
1 tsp sugar
1 tsp oregano
½ tsp thyme

12 link sausages (Italian sweet sausages may be used as well as American breakfast links)

SAUSAGES WITH RATATOUILLE (*French*)

Preparation . . .

1. Assemble and prepare all ingredients.

Cooking . . .

2. In 6-quart casserole, heat oil and cook onion and garlic for 5 minutes. Add eggplant and cook for 5 minutes. Add peppers and cook for 5 minutes. Add zucchini and cook for 5 minutes.
3. Add tomatoes and seasonings; simmer, covered, for 15 minutes. If vegetables look dry, add some tomato liquid.

At this point you may stop and continue later.

4. Simmer sausages in boiling water to cover for 10 minutes. Drain well and add them to simmering vegetable mixture. Continue cooking, covered, for 15 minutes, stirring occasionally.

TONGUE WITH CRANBERRIES—MAISON (*American*)

Serves 6
Doubles
Refrigerates

TOTAL TIME:
about 45 minutes
(30 minutes preparation,
15 minutes cooking)

You will need . . .

1 pre-cooked, ready-to-eat
beef tongue (2 lbs. or more)

1 can beef bouillon
1 cup packed brown sugar
1 1-lb. package fresh cranberries
4 Tbs butter
½ tsp ground clove
½ tsp salt
Grated rind and juice of 1 lemon

Chopped fresh parsley
Lemon slices

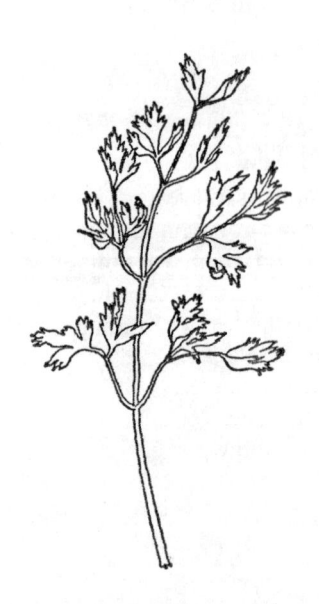

Serve with . . .
rice
creamed spinach with
horseradish (*American*)
sponge pudding (*American*)
Wine suggestions:
red Bordeaux,
domestic claret

TONGUE WITH CRANBERRIES–MAISON (*American*)

Preparation . . .

1. Assemble and prepare all ingredients.

2. In 6-quart casserole, combine these eight ingredients. Bring to boil; reduce heat and simmer, covered, until cranberries burst.

   At this point you may stop and continue later.

Cooking . . .

3. Slice tongue. Add to casserole, spooning cranberry mixture over. Simmer gently for 15 minutes. Garnish with parsley and serve with lemon slices.

   The dish is especially good prepared with fresh calf's tongue. Allow one tongue per serving. Simmer, covered, for 2 hours in water seasoned with salt, 3 stalks celery with leaves, 8 pepper corns. Drain, cool, skin the tongues and proceed as per step #2. If fresh cranberries are unavailable use 1 1-lb. can *whole* cranberry sauce, 1 packet dried beef bouillon powder and ¼ cup brown sugar.

TRIPE WITH CARROTS AND ONIONS (*French*)

Serves 6 to 8
Doubles
Refrigerates
Freezes

TOTAL TIME:
about 4¼ hours
(*45 minutes preparation,*
3½ hours cooking)

You will need . . .

3 lbs. honeycomb tripe
cut in bite-size pieces
(page 119)
6 carrots, sliced
3 stalks celery with tops, chopped
1 bunch parsley, chopped
1 tsp salt
1 tsp sugar
Water

18 white onions, peeled

3 Tbs butter
3 Tbs flour
1½ cups hot milk
1½ cups reserved tripe broth
Juice ½ lemon

Serve with . . .
muffins (American)
spinach salad (French)
pears with curry
(Middle Eastern)
Wine suggestions:
domestic or imported
red Burgundy

TRIPE WITH CARROTS AND ONIONS (*French*)

Preparation . . .

1. Assemble and prepare all ingredients.

Cooking . . .

2. In 6-quart casserole, combine first six ingredients; add water to cover and cook, covered, over low heat for 3 hours, or until tripe is tender.

3. Add onions to casserole and cook, covered, for about 12 minutes, or until they are just tender.

   At this point you may stop and continue later.

4. Strain contents of casserole through colander, reserving broth.
5. In casserole, melt butter and add flour, stirring; add milk and reserved broth, cooking until sauce thickens. Add tripe and onion mixture and heat through, stirring in lemon juice.

TRIPE WITH HOMINY (*Mexican*)

Serves 6
Doubles
Refrigerates
Freezes
Prepare a day in advance

TOTAL TIME:
about 3¾ hours
(*30 minutes preparation,*
3¼ hours cooking)

You will need . . .

3 lbs. honeycomb tripe
cut in bite-size pieces (page 119)
1 calf's foot *or* 2 pig's knuckles
4 cloves garlic, split
2 large onions, chopped
3 stalks celery with tops, chopped
1 Tbs salt
1 tsp sugar
1 tsp ground coriander
1 Tbs chili powder
¼ tsp each:
marjoram, rosemary, thyme
½ tsp pepper
Water

6 carrots, very thinly sliced

1 2-lb. can whole hominy,
well drained
Juice of 1 lemon

Serve with . . .
oatmeal-raisin bread
(*American*)
Caesar salad (*American*)
Wine suggestions:
domestic or imported
red Burgundy

TRIPE WITH HOMINY (*Mexican*)

Preparation . . .

1. Assemble and prepare all ingredients.

Cooking . . .

2. In 6-quart casserole, combine tripe, calf's foot, garlic, onion, celery, and seasonings; add water to cover. Bring to boil, reduce heat and simmer, covered, for 3 hours, or until tripe is tender and meat falls from bones.

3. Stir in carrots, bring stew to full boil; remove from heat and allow to cool, covered; when cool, refrigerate.

   At this point you stop; continue the next day.

4. Remove and discard fat and bones from cold casserole. Reheat, adding hominy and lemon juice; correct seasoning.

Main Dishes made with Poultry

Poultry, ideal for family meal or entertaining, is among the more reasonably priced meats at your supermarket, it is easily prepared, "holds" well, and is generally popular.

Casserole-cooked poultry requires only light surgery to separate meat from bone. Even for buffet meals, if a sitting-down place is provided, it is a welcome main dish.

Casseroles made with Chicken

The following recipes, calling for young chicken (fryers or broilers—not stewing fowl), list "serving pieces of chicken" so that you may choose your preferred portions. I eschew breasts for less expensive legs, which I find tastier. But as none of these dishes list specifically light *or* dark meat, it is a matter of choice.

In each instance browning the chicken is suggested; poultry dishes taste better if so treated. Browning the chicken may always be done in advance—and then the pieces may be refrigerated or frozen. However, experimentation and frequent lack of time have shown that browning poultry is not absolutely necessary. These recipes are successful when this step is omitted; in this case use the required butter or oil to grease casserole.

Recipes for the suggested side dishes given with each main dish may be found elsewhere in the book.

CHICKEN WITH ARTICHOKE HEARTS AND PEANUTS
(American)

Serves 6
Doubles
Refrigerates
Freezes

TOTAL TIME:
about 1½ hours
(30 minutes preparation,
1 hour cooking)

You will need . . .

3 Tbs butter
Serving-pieces of chicken
for 6 persons
2 packages frozen artichoke hearts
1 can cream of mushroom soup
½ cup coarsely chopped peanuts

1 cup sour cream

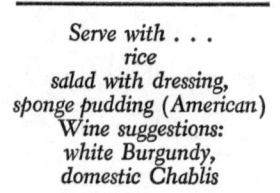

Serve with . . .
rice
salad with dressing,
sponge pudding (American)
Wine suggestions:
white Burgundy,
domestic Chablis

CHICKEN WITH ARTICHOKE HEARTS AND PEANUTS
(*American*)

Preparation . . .

1. Assemble and prepare all ingredients.
2. In 6-quart casserole, melt butter and brown chicken. Over the layer of chicken pieces, arrange artichoke hearts. Spoon mushroom soup over all and top with sprinkling of peanuts. (If quantity of recipe is increased, repeat layers as necessary.)

   At this point you may stop and continue later.

Cooking . . .

3. Bake, covered, at 350° for 1 hour, or until chicken is tender.

4. Before serving, spoon over sour cream and allow to heat through.

CHICKEN WITH APRICOTS AND RICE (*Middle Eastern*)

Serves 6
Doubles
Refrigerates

TOTAL TIME:
about 1½ hours
(30 minutes preparation,
1 hour cooking)

You will need . . .

3 Tbs oil
Serving-pieces of chicken
for 6 persons

1 onion, chopped
½ tsp ground allspice
¾ tsp turmeric
¼ tsp pepper
½ tsp ground cumin
1 tsp sugar
1½ tsp salt
1 Tbs ginger root, chopped
(preserved will do)

1 cup raw natural rice
¾ cup dried apricots, chopped

2½ cups chicken broth, boiling

Serve with . . .
zucchini with tomatoes
(Syrian)
pears with curry
(Middle Eastern)
Wine suggestions:
domestic or imported
vin rosé

CHICKEN WITH APRICOTS AND RICE (*Middle Eastern*)

Preparation . . .

1. Assemble and prepare all ingredients.
2. In 6-quart casserole, heat oil; brown chicken. Remove.
3. To pan juices, add onion and seasonings; cook until onion is translucent.
4. Add rice, stirring to coat with oil. Add apricots. Replace chicken.

    At this point you may stop and continue later.

Cooking . . .

5. Add broth and bake, covered, at 350° for 1 hour, or until chicken and rice are tender and liquid is absorbed. (More liquid may be added if necessary.)

    If desired, more than 1 cup of rice may be used. Allow ½ cup broth for the apricots; for whatever measure of rice, double quantity of broth.

CHICKEN WITH CURRY AND BUTTERMILK (Syrian)

Serves 6
Doubles
Refrigerates

TOTAL TIME:
about 3½ hours
(30 minutes preparation,
2 hours marinating,
1 hour cooking)

You will need . . .

1 cup buttermilk
2 cloves garlic, crushed
Serving-pieces of chicken
for 6 persons

4 Tbs oil
2 onions, chopped
2 cloves garlic, chopped
1½ tsp salt
1 tsp sugar
¾ tsp powdered ginger
½ tsp powdered cloves

1 Tbs curry powder (or more, to taste)

Serve with . . .
rice with orange and thyme
(American)
water cress and mushroom
salad (American)
peaches with red wine
(French)
Wine suggestions:
domestic or imported
dry sauterne

CHICKEN WITH CURRY AND BUTTERMILK (Syrian)

Preparation . . .

1. Assemble and prepare all ingredients.
2. Combine buttermilk and garlic, stirring. Add chicken and let marinate for 2 hours.
3. In 6-quart casserole, heat oil; add onion, garlic, and seasonings; cook, stirring, until onion is translucent.
4. Reduce heat, add curry powder, and cook gently, stirring, for 5 minutes.

   At this point you may stop and continue later.

Cooking . . .

5. To casserole, add buttermilk marinade, stirring. When ingredients are well blended, add chicken. Cook, covered, at 350° for 1 hour, or until chicken is tender.

CHICKEN WITH FIGS (*Middle Eastern*)

Serves 6
Doubles
Refrigerates

TOTAL TIME:
about 1½ hours
(30 minutes preparation,
1 hour cooking)

You will need . . .

3 Tbs butter
Serving-pieces of chicken
for 6 persons

3 Tbs flour
2 cups sour cream
1 tsp salt
¼ tsp white pepper
1 cup water
Grated rind and juice of 1 lemon

12 dried figs, quartered

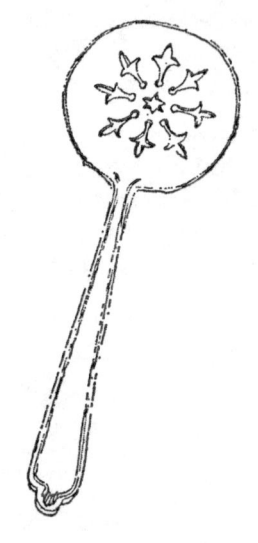

Serve with . . .
bulgur (Middle Eastern)
zucchini with tomatoes
(Syrian)
peaches with curry
(Middle Eastern)
Wine suggestions:
Neuchâtel,
domestic Chablis

CHICKEN WITH FIGS (*Middle Eastern*)

Preparation . . .

1. Assemble and prepare all ingredients.
2. In 6-quart casserole, melt butter and brown chicken. Remove.

3. Mix flour with pan juices. Remove from heat; stir in sour cream, salt, pepper, water, lemon juice and rind.

Cooking . . .

4. Add chicken and simmer, covered, for 40 minutes.

    At this point you may stop and continue later.

5. Add figs and cook for 20 minutes longer, or until chicken is tender.

CHICKEN WITH GINGER AND OLIVES (*Malayan*)

Serves 6
Doubles
Refrigerates

TOTAL TIME:
about 1½ hours
(30 minutes preparation,
1 hour cooking)

You will need . . .

4 Tbs oil
Serving-pieces of chicken
for 6 persons

½ cup orange juice
1 tsp powdered ginger
1 Tbs ginger root, chopped
(preserved will do)
1 tsp salt
1 tsp sugar
1 clove garlic, crushed
1 tsp turmeric

1 8-oz. can pitted ripe
(black) olives, halved
1 can water chestnuts,
drained and sliced
1 cup dry white wine

2 Tbs cornstarch
2 Tbs water

Serve with . . .
brown rice with scallions
and currants (American)
salad with dressing
grapes with sour cream
(American)
Wine suggestions:
domestic or imported
Rhine wine

CHICKEN WITH GINGER AND OLIVES (*Malayan*)

Preparation . . .

1. Assemble and prepare all ingredients.
2. In 6-quart casserole, heat oil; brown chicken.

3. Add these seven ingredients; reduce heat.

Cooking . . .

4. Add olives and water chestnuts, pour wine over all. Cook, covered, at 350° for 1 hour, or until chicken is tender.

   At this point you may stop and continue later.

5. Remove chicken from simmering casserole to warm plate. Combine cornstarch and water, add to casserole and cook over high heat, stirring, until sauce thickens. Return chicken pieces to casserole.

CHICKEN WITH LEMON AND SOUR CREAM (*Rumanian*)

Serves 6
Doubles
Refrigerates

TOTAL TIME:
about 1½ hours
(*30 minutes preparation,*
1 hour cooking)

You will need . . .

4 Tbs butter
Serving-pieces of chicken
for 6 persons

3 Tbs flour
2 cups sour cream
1½ tsp salt
¼ tsp white pepper

12 mushrooms, sliced
2 Tbs parsley, chopped
4 scallions, chopped
Grated rind 1 lemon

2 or 3 Tbs lemon juice

Serve with . . .
barley casserole
(*Middle Eastern*)
onions with honey
(*Flemish*)
dried fruit compote
or
vegetable casserole
(*Rumanian*)
salad with dressing
and feta cheese
rice pudding (*Greek*)
Wine suggestions:
Vouvray,
domestic dry sauterne

CHICKEN WITH LEMON AND SOUR CREAM (*Rumanian*)

Preparation . . .

1. Assemble and prepare all ingredients.
2. In 6-quart casserole, melt butter and brown chicken; remove.

3. Stir flour into pan juices; add sour cream, salt and pepper; mix well and simmer about 3 minutes.

4. Stir in these four ingredients; add chicken and spoon sauce over it.

    At this point you may stop and continue later.

Cooking . . .

5. Cook, covered, at 350° for 1 hour, or until chicken is tender. Just before serving, stir in lemon juice.

CHICKEN WITH LEMON AND TARRAGON–MAISON
(*American*)

Serves 6
Doubles
Refrigerates
Freezes

TOTAL TIME:
about 1½ hours
(30 minutes preparation,
1 hour cooking)

You will need . . .

3 Tbs butter
Serving-pieces of chicken
for 6 persons

1 can cream of mushroom soup
Juice and grated rind of 1 lemon
½ tsp salt
¼ tsp white pepper
1½ tsp dried tarragon

Serve with . . .
rice
onions with honey
(Flemish)
spinach salad with orange
and bacon (American)
Wine suggestions:
domestic or imported
Chablis

CHICKEN WITH LEMON AND TARRAGON—MAISON
(*American*)

Preparation . . .

1. Assemble and prepare all ingredients.
2. In 6-quart casserole, melt butter and brown chicken.

3. Combine these six ingredients and pour over chicken.

At this point you may stop and continue later.

Cooking . . .

4. Bake, covered, at 350° for 1 hour, or until chicken is tender.

CHICKEN WITH MANDARIN ORANGES AND MARASCHINO CHERRIES (*Middle Eastern*)

Serves 6
Doubles
Refrigerates

TOTAL TIME:
about 1 ¾ hours
(45 minutes preparation,
1 hour cooking)

You will need . . .

Serving-pieces of chicken
for 6 persons
Flour
Salt
Pepper
1 tsp paprika
4 Tbs oil
1 clove garlic, minced

½ cup chicken broth
2 Tbs cider vinegar
Syrup from mandarin oranges
and maraschino cherries
(see below)
1 Tbs brown sugar
¼ tsp rosemary

1 Tbs cornstarch
1 Tbs water

1 11-oz. can mandarin orange
sections (drained—see above)
1 4-oz. jar maraschino cherries
(drained—see above)
½ cup seedless raisins

Serve with . . .
rice
salad with dressing
and cheese of your choice
Wine suggestions:
Neuchâtel or
domestic Rhine wine

CHICKEN WITH MANDARIN ORANGES AND MARASCHINO CHERRIES (*Middle Eastern*)

Preparation . . .

1. Assemble and prepare all ingredients.
2. Dredge chicken in seasoned flour.//
3. In 6-quart casserole, heat oil; add garlic and then chicken; brown well.

   At this point you may stop and continue later.

Cooking . . .

4. Combine liquids, sugar, and rosemary. Add to casserole and bake, covered, at 350° for 1 hour, or until chicken is tender. Remove chicken to warm plate.
5. Combine cornstarch and water and add to casserole, stirring to thicken.
6. Add fruits to sauce in casserole and heat through. Return chicken to casserole.

CHICKEN WITH PAPRIKA (*Austrian*)

*Serves 6
Doubles
Refrigerates
Freezes*

TOTAL TIME:
*about 1½ hours
(30 minutes preparation,
1 hour cooking)*

You will need . . .

4 Tbs butter
1 onion, chopped
2 tsp paprika (or more to taste)
Serving-pieces of chicken
for 6 persons

1 Tbs flour
2 cups consommé
1 Tbs heavy cream or
evaporated milk

1 cup sour cream
Chopped fresh dill (dried will do)

*Serve with . . .
bulgur (Middle Eastern)
zucchini with tomatoes
(Syrian)
salad with dressing
and cheese of your choice
Wine suggestions:
domestic or imported
Rhine wine*

CHICKEN WITH PAPRIKA (*Austrian*)

Preparation . . .

1. Assemble and prepare all ingredients.
2. In 6-quart casserole, melt butter and cook onion until translucent. Add paprika and mix well. Add chicken and brown.

Cooking . . .

3. To flour add a little consommé, stirring until smooth. Combine with remaining consommé and cream; add to casserole and bake, covered, at 350° for 1 hour, or until chicken is tender.

   At this point you may stop and continue later.

4. Remove chicken to warm plate. Blend sour cream with pan juices; do not allow to boil. Return chicken to casserole and garnish with dill.

CHICKEN WITH PRUNES AND SHERRY—MAISON
(*American*)

Serves 6
Doubles
Refrigerates

TOTAL TIME:
about 1½ hours
(30 minutes preparation,
1 hour cooking)

You will need . . .

Serving-pieces of chicken
for 6 persons
Flour
Salt
Pepper
4 Tbs butter

2 onions, chopped
12 or 18 dried prunes, pitted

1 cup dry sherry
1 cup orange juice

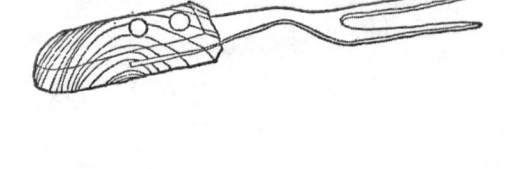

Serve with . . .
muffins (American)
salad with dressing
sponge pudding (American)
Wine suggestions:
domestic or imported
vin rosé

CHICKEN WITH PRUNES AND SHERRY—MAISON
(*American*)

Preparation . . .

1. Assemble and prepare all ingredients.
2. Dredge chicken in seasoned flour. In 6-quart casserole, melt butter and brown chicken.
3. To casserole add layer of onions, then prunes. Repeat layers as necessary.

   At this point you may stop and continue later.

Cooking . . .

4. Add liquids to casserole and cook, covered, at 350° for 1 hour, or until chicken is tender. Remove cover during final minutes of cooking so that sauce thickens.

CHICKEN WITH SHERRY AND CREAM (*Spanish*)

Serves 6
Doubles
Refrigerates

TOTAL TIME:
about 1½ hours
(*30 minutes preparation,*
1 hour cooking)

You will need . . .

Serving-pieces of chicken
for 6 persons
Flour
Salt
Pepper
¾ tsp paprika

4 Tbs butter
½ lb. mushrooms, sliced

1 cup light cream
¾ cup sherry

Serve with . . .
rice
spinach salad
(*French*)
pears with red wine
(*French*)
Wine suggestions:
domestic or imported
vin rosé

CHICKEN WITH SHERRY AND CREAM (*Spanish*)

Preparation . . .

1. Assemble and prepare all ingredients.
2. Dredge chicken in seasoned flour.

3. In 6-quart casserole, melt butter and brown chicken. Add mushrooms and cook for 5 minutes.

    At this point you may stop and continue later.

Cooking . . .

4. Combine liquids, pour over chicken; bake, covered, at 350° for 1 hour, or until chicken is tender.

    If desired, the grated rind and juice of 1 lemon may be added with mushrooms.

CHICKEN WITH SWEET WINE (*Haitian*)

Serves 6
Doubles
Refrigerates

TOTAL TIME:
about 1¾ hours
(*30 minutes preparation,*
1¼ hours cooking)

You will need . . .

4 Tbs oil
Serving-pieces of chicken
for 6 persons

1 cup water
1 clove garlic, mashed
¼ tsp pepper
1 tsp oregano
2 tsp salt
1 tsp vinegar

12 white onions, peeled
12 green olives, pitted
12 dried prunes, pitted
⅓ cup white raisins
2 bay leaves, broken
6 small potatoes, peeled and diced

1½ cups muscatel wine
¼ cup sugar
2″ or 3″ cinnamon stick

Serve with . . .
bread en casserole,
Variation III (*Italian*)
spinach salad (*French*)
blueberry duff (*American*)
or
gingerbread (*American*)
Wine suggestions:
white Burgundy,
domestic dry sauterne

CHICKEN WITH SWEET WINE (*Haitian*)

Preparation . . .

1. Assemble and prepare all ingredients.
2. In 6-quart casserole, heat oil; brown chicken.
3. Mix water with garlic, seasonings, and vinegar; pour over chicken.

Cooking . . .

4. Add these six ingredients, bring to boil, reduce heat, and simmer, covered, for 15 minutes.

5. Mix wine with sugar and add to casserole, together with cinnamon stick; simmer, covered, for 15 minutes.

   At this point you may stop and continue later.

6. Remove cover and continue cooking for 30 minutes (or place, uncovered, in 350° oven for 30 minutes). Sauce will thicken a bit during final cooking.

CHICKEN WITH WHITE PORT AND CORIANDER
(Portuguese)

Serves 6
Doubles
Refrigerates

TOTAL TIME:
about 1½ hours
(30 minutes preparation,
1 hour cooking)

You will need . . .

4 Tbs butter
Serving-pieces of chicken
for 6 persons

2 Tbs flour
3 cloves garlic, split
½ tsp salt
¼ tsp white pepper
1½ tsp ground coriander

1½ cups white port wine
Hot water

1 cup heavy cream

Serve with . . .
rice with saffron and
tomatoes
salad with dressing
jellied sherry (Spanish)
Wine suggestions:
domestic or imported
vin rosé

CHICKEN WITH WHITE PORT AND CORIANDER
(*Portuguese*)

Preparation . . .

1. Assemble and prepare all ingredients.
2. In 6-quart casserole, melt butter and brown chicken; remove.
3. Mix flour with pan juices; add garlic and seasonings and blend. Replace chicken.

Cooking . . .

4. Add wine and enough water just to cover. Bring to boil; reduce heat and simmer, covered, for 40 minutes, or until chicken is tender.

   At this point you may stop and continue later.

5. Remove chicken pieces from simmering casserole to warm dish. Reduce liquid to about 1¼ cups. Stir in cream and simmer for 3 minutes (do not boil). Replace chicken.

OVEN-BARBECUED CHICKEN—MAISON (*American*)

Serves 6
Doubles
Refrigerates
Freezes

TOTAL TIME:
about 1½ hours
(30 minutes preparation,
1 hour cooking)

You will need . . .

1 cup flour
2 tsp salt
½ tsp pepper
2 tsp paprika
1 tsp sugar
Serving-pieces of chicken
for 6 persons

¼ lb. butter, melted

This and the following recipe are not cooked en casserole, but are so easy, quick, and successful, such good "holders," that they are offered as variations to casserole-cooked poultry. Both oven-barbecued and oven-fried chicken can be prepared well in advance—even put in the oven; just turn on the heat a good hour before serving.

½ cup onion, chopped fine
1 tsp salt
¼ tsp pepper
1 tsp sugar
1 Tbs cider vinegar
½ tsp chili powder
1 Tbs Worcestershire sauce
½ cup catsup
¼ cup water

Serve with . . .
spinach with sour cream
and horseradish (American)
potato salad (French)
peaches with red wine
(French)
Wine suggestions:
domestic or imported
Rhine wine

OVEN-BARBECUED CHICKEN—MAISON (*American*)

Preparation . . .

1. Assemble and prepare all ingredients.
2. Mix flour with seasonings and dredge chicken.

3. Dip chicken pieces into butter and arrange them on a lightly oiled cookie sheet.

    At this point you may stop and continue later.

Cooking . . .

4. Combine these nine ingredients to make a sauce. Bake chicken at 350° for one hour; turn the pieces and add sauce after the first thirty minutes.

OVEN-FRIED CHICKEN—MAISON (*American*)

*Serves 6
Doubles
Refrigerates
Freezes*

TOTAL TIME:
*about 1¼ hours
(15 minutes preparation,
1 hour cooking)*

You will need . . .

Serving-pieces of chicken
for 6 persons
Oil
Cornflake crumbs
Salt
Pepper

This recipe resulted from a quest for chicken tasting like Austrian backhändl, *but omitting the heavy batter and deep-frying process.*

*Serve with . . .
spinach with sour cream
and horseradish (American)
potato salad (French)
pears with red wine
(French)
Wine suggestions:
domestic or imported
Chablis or Rhine wine*

OVEN-FRIED CHICKEN—MAISON (*American*)

Preparation . . .

1. Assemble and prepare all ingredients.
2. Coat chicken with oil and encrust with seasoned crumbs by dredging thoroughly. Arrange chicken on lightly-oiled cookie sheet.

   At this point you may stop and continue later.

Cooking . . .

3. Bake at 350° for 1 hour, or until chicken is tender.

   For an Italian flavor use olive oil and crumbs seasoned with dried oregano. (Crumbs may also be seasoned with parsley, marjoram, or thyme.)

CHICKEN LOAF—MAISON (*American*)

Serves 6
Refrigerates

TOTAL TIME:
about 2½ hours
(*30 minutes preparation,*
2 hours cooking)

You will need . . .

Table leavings of chicken
(bones, etc.) plus backs,
necks, wing tips, giblets
1 bay leaf, broken
1 tsp salt
½ tsp pepper
1 tsp sugar
¼ tsp thyme
Water

1 onion, grated
1 clove garlic, minced
Reserved chicken broth, heated

3 Tbs mayonnaise
½ tsp salt

1 package unflavored gelatin
¼ cup cold water
1 cup reserved broth, boiling

2 Tbs chopped chives

Serve with . . .
muffins (*American*)
Caesar salad (*American*)
seedless grapes with sour
cream (*American*)
Wine suggestions:
domestic or imported
Chablis

CHICKEN LOAF—MAISON (*American*)

Preparation . . .

1. Assemble and prepare all ingredients.

Cooking . . .

2. In 6-quart casserole, combine chicken bits, seasonings, and water just to cover. Bring to boil; reduce heat, and simmer, covered, for 2 hours. Drain, reserving broth. Allow chicken pieces to cool.

   At this point you may stop and continue later.

3. Remove meat and skin from bones and reserve; discard bones.
4. In container of electric blender, combine reserved chicken pieces, onion, garlic, and enough reserved broth to allow blender knives to work. Reduce contents of container to a paste (low speed).
5. Add mayonnaise and salt.

6. Moisten gelatin in water; add to boiling broth and dissolve. Add mixture to container, cover, and blend on low speed for 15 seconds.
7. Add chives and stir. Pour into loaf pan and chill to set.

   If desired, ⅓ cup ripe (black) or stuffed green olives, coarsely chopped, may be added with the chives.

Casseroles made with Duck

Although the majority of recipes in this book are designed to serve six persons, those for casseroles made with duck serve four. Duck seems to divide naturally into four serving pieces—two wings with breasts and two legs with thighs. Use a four- to five-pound duck for four servings. I prefer the frozen variety, completely dressed and cleaned. Once thawed, it is easily sectioned and ready to cook. As duck tends to be greasy, I cut away as much yellow fat as possible before cooking; and I puncture the skin with a fork to allow the duck to drain.

Recipes for the suggested side dishes given with each main dish may be found elsewhere in the book.

DUCK WITH APPLES (*French*)

Serves 4
Doubles
Refrigerates

TOTAL TIME:
about 2 hours
(30 minutes preparation,
1½ hours cooking)

You will need . . .

4 Tbs butter
1 duck cut in serving pieces
(page 177)

6 tart apples, pared, cored, and sliced
2 large onions, sliced
1 tsp salt
½ tsp pepper

¼ cup cognac

Serve with . . .
bread en casserole
(French)
braised fennel (French)
pears with red wine
(French)
Wine suggestions:
red Bordeaux or domestic claret

DUCK WITH APPLES (*French*)

Preparation . . .

1. Assemble and prepare all ingredients.
2. In 6-quart casserole, melt butter and brown duck well; remove. With remaining grease wipe sides of casserole; discard excess fat.
3. In casserole, arrange layers of apple and onion. Season. Place duck pieces on top, skin side up.

At this point you may stop and continue later.

Cooking . . .

1. In saucepan, warm and ignite cognac; pour over contents of casserole. When flame dies cover casserole and bake at 325° for 1½ hours, or until duck is tender.

DUCK WITH GINGER (*Chinese*)

Serves 4
Doubles
Refrigerates

TOTAL TIME:
about 2 hours
(30 minutes preparation,
1½ hours cooking)

You *will need* . . .

4 Tbs oil
1 duck cut in serving pieces
(page 177)

2 cans water chestnuts, sliced
2 cans bamboo shoots
6 scallions, chopped
(with as much green as possible)
2 tsp fresh ginger root, chopped
(preserved will do)
¼ lb. mushrooms, sliced
4 stalks celery, chopped

5 cups water, boiling

4 tsp cornstarch
3 Tbs soy sauce
3 Tbs sherry
1 tsp sugar

Serve with . . .
rice
sweet and sour
vegetables (Chinese)
Wine suggestions:
domestic or imported
Burgundy

DUCK WITH GINGER (*Chinese*)

Preparation . . .

1. Assemble and prepare all ingredients.
2. In 6-quart casserole, heat oil; add duck, and brown well. Discard excess fat.

3. Add these six ingredients.

At this point you may stop and continue later.

Cooking . . .

4. Pour boiling water over all, cover, and bake at 350° for 1½ hours, or until duck is tender. More water may be added if necessary.
5. Combine these four ingredients, add to the casserole, stirring gently to blend and thicken.

DUCK WITH OLIVES AND MUSHROOMS (*Spanish*)

Serves 4
Doubles
Refrigerates

TOTAL TIME:
about 2½ hours
(30 minutes preparation,
2 hours cooking)

You will need . . .

½ tsp salt
½ tsp pepper
½ tsp paprika
1 duck cut in serving pieces
(page 177)

3 Tbs butter
3 large carrots, sliced
3 large stalks celery, chopped
2 large onions, chopped

1 cup tomato juice
1 bay leaf, broken

⅓ cup green olives, sliced
(stuffed olives add color)
½ lb. mushrooms, sliced

Serve with . . .
rice
salad with dressing
jellied sherry (Spanish)
Wine suggestions:
red Côtes du Rhone,
domestic claret

DUCK WITH OLIVES AND MUSHROOMS (*Spanish*)

Preparation . . .

1. Assemble and prepare all ingredients.
2. Mix together seasonings and sprinkle duck.

Cooking . . .

3. In 6-quart casserole, arrange duck pieces with skin side up. Bake, uncovered, at 325° for 1½ hours. Drain off excess fat.
4. In saucepan, melt butter, add carrots, celery, and onion; cook until onion is translucent.
5. Add tomato juice and bay leaf to vegetables and cook, covered, for 20 minutes, or until vegetables are tender.
6. Add olives and mushrooms to casserole, then contents of saucepan.

   At this point you may stop and continue later.
7. Bake, covered, at 325° for 30 minutes.

Main Dishes made with Fish or Seafood

There is a cleanness about fish and seafood which makes preparing them a pleasure; frequently sold pan-ready, they are as reasonably priced as other main-dish foods; they are light, non-fattening, and quickly cooked.

The following recipes for filets, for shrimp, and for scallops may be readied ahead of time. The cooking of fish and seafood is, generally, a last-minute affair.

Main Dishes made with Fish Filets

These four recipes are designed for boneless filets of sole or flounder. Allow one filet per person. I find them easier to serve if they are rolled and skewered with toothpicks before cooking. If you prefer, the filet may be cut in two lengthwise halves and each piece skewered separately.

Recipes for the suggested side dishes given with each main dish may be found elsewhere in the book.

FILETS WITH CHEESE AND SHERRY (*American*)

Serves 6
Doubles

TOTAL TIME:
about 45 minutes
(20 minutes preparation,
25 minutes cooking)

You will need . . .

1 filet per serving (page 187)
Flour
Salt
Pepper
1 pint half-and-half cream

½ cup parsley, chopped
1 package (8 slices)
mild processed cheese
Paprika

½ cup sherry

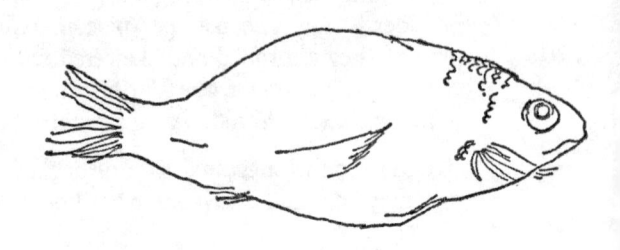

Serve with . . .
brown rice with
scallions and currants
(*American*)
wilted lettuce salad
(*American*)
blueberry duff (*American*)
Wine suggestions:
domestic or imported
Rhine wine

FILETS WITH CHEESE AND SHERRY (American)

Preparation . . .

1. Assemble and prepare all ingredients.
2. Dredge filets in seasoned flour. In lightly buttered baking dish, arrange filets flat on bottom. Add cream to cover.

3. Sprinkle parsley over fish. Add layer of cheese, one slice deep. Pour over remaining cream. Sprinkle with paprika.

   At this point you may stop and continue later.

Cooking . . .

4. Bake, uncovered, at 400° for 15 minutes. Add sherry and bake 5 minutes longer, or until fish flakes easily.

FILETS WITH ORANGE SAUCE—MAISON (*French*)

Serves 6
Doubles

TOTAL TIME:
about 1 hour
(30 minutes preparation,
20 minutes cooking)

You will need . . .

1 filet per serving (page 187)
Butter

4 Tbs butter
2 Tbs flour
1 cup orange juice
Grated rind of 1 orange
½ tsp salt
⅛ tsp white pepper

An unusually satisfying fish dish because of the freshness the orange gives.

Serve with . . .
(Please note: if the following menu is used, cook fish for only 15 minutes at 425°, *to accommodate baking of gougère.*)
  braised fennel (French)
  gougère (French)
  spinach salad (French)
  and French cheese of your choice
  Wine suggestions:
  Neuchâtel,
  domestic Chablis

FILETS WITH ORANGE SAUCE—MAISON (*French*)

Preparation . . .

1. Assemble and prepare all ingredients.
2. Arrange filets in lightly buttered baking dish.
3. In saucepan, melt butter and stir in flour; add orange juice, rind, and seasonings; cook, stirring, until sauce thickens. Pour evenly over filets.

   At this point you may stop and continue later.

Cooking . . .

4. Bake, uncovered, at 400° for 20 minutes, or until fish flakes easily. If desired, ½ clove garlic, crushed, may be added when making sauce.

FILETS WITH PEACHES AND GINGER (*Dutch*)

Serves 6
Doubles

TOTAL TIME:
about 1 hour
(*40 minutes preparation,
20 minutes cooking*)

You will need . . .

¼ lb. butter
1 filet per serving (page 187)

1 1-lb. can sliced peaches, drained
(reserve juice)

1 Tbs ginger root, chopped
(preserved will do)
Reserved peach juice
1 tsp powdered ginger
¼ cup water
¼ tsp salt
⅛ tsp white pepper

2 Tbs water
1 Tbs cornstarch
2 Tbs lemon juice

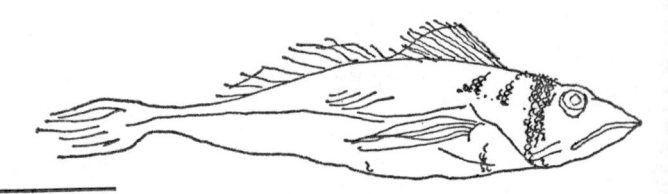

Serve with . . .
muffins (American)
green beans with sour cream
and dill (American)
salad with dressing
sponge pudding (American)
Wine suggestions:
Vouvray,
domestic Rhine wine

FILETS WITH PEACHES AND GINGER (*Dutch*)

Preparation . . .

1. Assemble and prepare all ingredients.
2. In small saucepan, cook butter until it browns; with a little of it, lightly grease a baking dish. Arrange filets in baking dish and pour over remaining butter. Arrange peach slices on fish.
3. In small saucepan, combine ginger root, reserved peach juice, water, and seasonings. Bring to boil and simmer, covered, for 20 minutes. Remove from heat.

At this point you may stop and continue later.

Cooking . . .

4. Bake filets, uncovered, at 400° for 20 minutes, or until fish flakes easily.
5. Meanwhile, combine water, cornstarch, and lemon juice. Add to ginger sauce and cook until thickened; pour over fish.

FILETS WITH WHITE WINE AND CUMIN (*Greek*)

Serves 6
Doubles

TOTAL TIME:
about 40 minutes
(20 minutes preparation,
20 minutes cooking)

You will need . . .

2 Tbs oil
1 onion, thinly sliced
½ lemon, thinly sliced
Parsley sprigs
1 bay leaf, crushed
1 filet per serving (page 187)

4 Tbs olive oil
½ cup dry white wine
1 tsp salt
1½ tsp ground cumin

The recipe works well for halibut steak: 2 lbs. of fish will serve 6 persons and the quantity may be doubled, if desired; allow 40 minutes baking time at 350° for the heavier fish.

Serve with . . .
carrots with nutmeg and honey (Flemish)
salad with dressing
rice pudding (Greek)
Wine suggestions:
Moselle, domestic Chablis

FILETS WITH WHITE WINE AND CUMIN (*Greek*)

Preparation . . .

1. Assemble and prepare all ingredients.
2. Lightly coat baking dish with oil. On bottom, arrange onion, lemon, parsley sprigs, and bay leaf; on top, arrange filets.

3. Shake together these four ingredients.

At this point you may stop and continue later.

Cooking . . .

4. Pour olive oil mixture over fish; bake, tightly covered, at 400° for 20 minutes, or until fish flakes easily.

Main Dishes made with Scallops

There are two kinds of scallops—bay and sea. Bay scallops are smaller, sweeter, tenderer; they take less time to cook and cost considerably more than their ocean-dwelling relatives. Most exchequers require more frequent use of sea scallops which, if extra large, may be cut in halves or quarters. Both varieties toughen and dry if cooked either at too high a temperature or for too long a time. For other dishes using scallops, see pp. 218 and 220.

Recipes for the suggested side dishes given with each main dish may be found elsewhere in the book.

SCALLOPS WITH RICE (*Greek*)

Serves 6
Doubles
Refrigerates
Freezes

TOTAL TIME:
about 1 hour
*(30 minutes preparation,
30 minutes cooking)*

You will need . . .

4 Tbs butter
2 onions, chopped

3 Tbs oil
1½ cups raw natural rice
1 cup fresh parsley, chopped
1½ tsp salt
¼ tsp pepper

½ cup dry white wine
¼ tsp thyme
1 bay leaf, crushed
1½ lbs. sea scallops, halved
Boiling water

Serve with . . .
onions with apples
(*Flemish*)
spinach salad (*French*)
individual chocolate mousse
(*French*)
Wine suggestions:
domestic or imported
Chablis

SCALLOPS WITH RICE (*Greek*)

Preparation . . .

1. Assemble and prepare all ingredients.
2. In 6-quart casserole, melt butter and cook onion until translucent. Remove and reserve.
3. In casserole, heat oil and cook rice until it is well coated and begins to turn golden. Add reserved onion, parsley, and seasonings. Cover.

   At this point you may stop and continue later.

4. In saucepan, heat wine with thyme and bay leaf. Add scallops and boiling water to cover. Reduce heat and simmer for 5 minutes. Remove and reserve scallops; strain and reserve broth.

Cooking . . .

5. Add boiling water to broth to yield 3 cups; pour over rice mixture, stir once, and bake, covered, at 350° for 20 minutes.
6. Stir in scallops and bake, covered, for 10 minutes longer.

SCALLOPS WITH WINE-AND-CHEESE SAUCE (*Greek*)

Serves 6
Doubles
Refrigerates

TOTAL TIME:
*about 45 minutes
(25 minutes preparation,
20 minutes cooking)*

You will need . . .

1½ lbs. sea scallops, halved
½ cup dry white wine
½ tsp salt
1 bay leaf, crushed
Dash cayenne
1 small onion, minced

3 Tbs butter
3 Tbs flour
½ cup heavy cream
1 cup grated cheese (cheddar for a hearty sauce; Meunster for a delicate one)

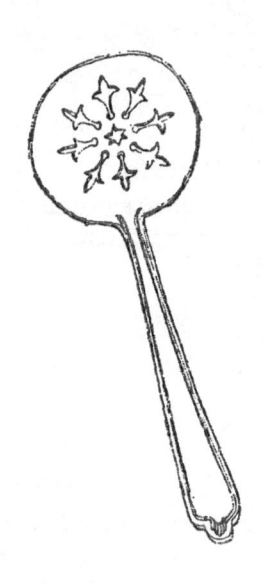

Serve with . . .
*zucchini with tomatoes
(Syrian)
bulgur salad
(Middle Eastern)
curried peaches
(Middle Eastern)
Wine suggestions:
domestic or imported
vin rosé*

SCALLOPS WITH WINE-AND-CHEESE SAUCE (*Greek*)

Preparation . . .

1. Assemble and prepare all ingredients.
2. In 6-quart casserole, combine scallops with wine, seasonings, and onion. Bring to boil; reduce heat and simmer, covered, for 10 minutes. Remove and reserve scallops. Strain and reserve broth.
3. In casserole, melt butter and add flour, stirring; add 1 cup of reserved broth and the cream, stirring until sauce is thickened. Add cheese, stirring until melted. Add scallops.

   At this point you may stop and continue later.

Cooking . . .

4. Bake, uncovered, at 350° for 20 minutes.

CLAMS WITH EGGPLANT (*American*)

*Serves 6
Doubles
Refrigerates
Freezes*

TOTAL TIME:
*about 1 hour
(30 minutes preparation,
30 minutes cooking)*

You will need . . .

2 medium eggplants

2 8-oz. cans minced clams
Heavy cream

3 Tbs butter
1 onion, chopped
½ green pepper, chopped
3 Tbs flour
3 Tbs parsley flakes
Paprika

*Serve with . . .
bulgur (Middle Eastern)
spinach salad with orange
and bacon (American)
Wine suggestions:
domestic or imported
Chablis*

CLAMS WITH EGGPLANT (*American*)

Preparation . . .

1. Assemble and prepare all ingredients.
2. Peel and cut eggplant into 1" cubes. Cook in boiling salted water for 10 minutes; drain.
3. Drain juice from clams and add cream to yield 2½ cups.
4. In 6-quart casserole, melt butter and cook onion and green pepper until translucent. Add flour, stirring to yield smooth paste. Add clam juice mixture, stirring until thickened. Add minced clams, eggplant, and parsley, stirring gently to blend the ingredients. Sprinkle with paprika.

At this point you may stop and continue later.

Cooking . . .

5. Bake, uncovered, at 350° for 30 minutes.

Main Dishes made with Shrimp

For best results, use fresh, uncooked shrimp. Shelling and deveining them is well worth the effort and not arduous if you use the gadget which shells and deveins in one operation. If you buy jumbo-size shrimp, cut them in half after cleaning. For most recipes, shrimps sold for "large" (not jumbo-giant) and cooked whole are most satisfactory, being frequently of sweeter flavor. Frozen shrimp are available and are adequate substitutes.

Recipes for the suggested side dishes given with each main dish may be found elsewhere in the book.

SHRIMP WITH BAMBOO SHOOTS (*Chinese*)

Serves 6
Doubles reasonably well
Refrigerates if necessary

TOTAL TIME:
about 1 hour
(45 minutes preparation,
15 minutes cooking)

You will need . . .

1½ lbs. raw shrimp,
shelled and deveined
4 tsp cornstarch
¾ tsp salt
3 Tbs sherry
3 Tbs oil

1 Tbs oil
1½ cups bamboo shoots

3 Tbs soy sauce
1½ tsp sugar
¾ tsp cornstarch
⅓ cup water

The special quality of Chinese dishes is their freshness of taste and crispness of texture coming from the rapidity with which they are cooked. For this reason, I have reservations about doubling, preferring to prepare double the ingredients called for by the recipe, but to cook the dish twice. Refrigerated Chinese dishes are edible, but have little of the fresh-crisp character of new-cooked ones.

Serve with . . .
rice
sweet-and-sour
vegetables (*Chinese*)
kumquat and leechee nut
compote (*Chinese*)
(*a good China tea, rather than wine, is the best accompaniment to Chinese food*)

SHRIMP WITH BAMBOO SHOOTS (Chinese)

Preparation . . .

1. Assemble and prepare all ingredients.

Cooking . . .

2. Dredge shrimp in mixture of cornstarch, salt, and sherry. Heat 6-quart casserole, add oil and cook shrimp for 3 minutes. Remove to absorbent paper.

3. Reheat casserole, add oil and then bamboo shoots, stirring until well coated with oil.
4. Combine soy sauce, sugar, cornstarch, and water; pour over bamboo shoots and cook, stirring, until sauce thickens. Add reserved shrimp and heat through.

   Variation I: omit bamboo shoots; substitute 3 cucumbers, peeled, quartered lengthwise, and cut in 2" pieces.

   Variation II: omit bamboo shoots; substitute 3 green peppers, seeded and cut in julienne strips.

   Variation III: use a combination of bamboo shoots, cucumber, and green pepper.

SHRIMP WITH COD FILETS AND RICE (*Spanish*)

Serves 6
Doubles
Refrigerates

TOTAL TIME:
about 1¼ hours
(45 minutes preparation,
30 minutes cooking)

You will need . . .

¼ cup olive oil
1 onion, chopped
2 cloves garlic, chopped
1 tsp salt
1 4-oz. can chopped pimento, drained

1 cup natural raw rice

1 8-oz. can minced clams, drained
Reserved clam juice
Water
1 package frozen artichoke hearts, thawed

1 lb. raw shrimp, shelled and deveined
1½ lbs. cod filet, cut in bite-size pieces

Serve with . . .
salad with dressing
jellied sherry (*Spanish*)
Wine suggestions:
domestic or imported
vin rosé

SHRIMP WITH COD FILETS AND RICE (Spanish)

Preparation . . .

1. Assemble and prepare all ingredients.
2. In 6-quart casserole, heat oil; add the next four ingredients, and cook until onion is translucent.
3. Add rice, stirring to coat well with oil.

   At this point you may stop and continue later.
4. Add clams. Combine clam juice and water to yield 2¼ cups and bring to boil.
5. Over contents of casserole arrange layer of artichoke hearts.

Cooking . . .

6. Add shrimp in a layer, then cod filet. Pour boiling clam juice-water mixture over all and bake, covered, at 350° for 30 minutes, or until fish flakes easily and rice is tender and liquid absorbed.

SHRIMP WITH CRABMEAT–I–MAISON (*American*)

Serves 6
Doubles
Refrigerates

TOTAL TIME:
about 1¼ hours
(*30 minutes preparation,
45 minutes cooking*)

You will need . . .

1 can frozen shrimp soup,
fully thawed, *un*diluted
1 10-oz. can Newburg sauce
4 scallions, chopped
1 8-oz. can pitted ripe (black)
olives, quartered
1 can pimentos, chopped
1 clove garlic, crushed
½ cup sherry
2 3-oz. cans mushrooms, drained
1 can water chestnuts,
drained and sliced
1 tsp sugar
¾ tsp salt
¼ tsp white pepper
½ lb. can crabmeat,
tendons removed
1 lb. frozen shrimp
Grated Parmesan cheese

Serve with . . .
barley (Middle Eastern)
*spinach salad with orange
and bacon (American)*
*Wine suggestions:
domestic or imported
dry sauterne*

SHRIMP WITH CRABMEAT–I–MAISON (*American*)

Preparation . . .

1. Assemble and prepare all ingredients.
2. In 6-quart casserole, toss together all ingredients. Sprinkle with cheese.

At this point you may stop and continue later.

Cooking . . .

3. Bake, uncovered, at 350° for 45 minutes to 1 hour.

SHRIMP WITH CRABMEAT–II (*American*)

Serves 6
Doubles
Refrigerates

TOTAL TIME:
about 1½ hours
(*30 minutes preparation,*
1 hour cooking)

You will need . . .

1½ lbs. crab meat
with tendons removed
1 lb. frozen shrimp
¼ green pepper, chopped
⅓ cup parsley, chopped
2 cups cooked rice
1½ cups mayonnaise
2 packages frozen peas
¾ tsp salt
⅓ tsp white pepper

Serve with . . .
muffins (*American*)
green beans with
sour cream and dill
(*American*)
sponge pudding
(*American*)
Wine suggestions:
white Burgundy,
domestic Chablis

SHRIMP WITH CRABMEAT—II (*American*)

Preparation . . .

1. Assemble and prepare all ingredients.
2. In lightly buttered 6-quart casserole, toss together all ingredients.

At this point you may stop and continue later.

Also, at this point dish may be refrigerated.

Cooking . . .

3. Bake, covered, at 350° for 1 hour.

SHRIMP GUMBO (*American*)

Serves 6
Doubles
Refrigerates

TOTAL TIME:
about 2¾ hours
(1 hour preparation,
1¾ hours cooking)

A traditional New Orleans dish, shrimp gumbo derives its taste and texture from the addition, before serving, of gumbo filé, a flavoring agent widely used in the South. Gumbo filé is powdered sassafras leaf; originally made by Choctaw Indians, who sold it to the French, its Indian name is kombo.

Serve with . . .
rice
peaches with red wine
(French)
Wine suggestions:
domestic or imported
Chablis

You will need . . .

1½ lbs. raw shrimp
2 bay leaves, broken
½ tsp thyme
½ tsp pepper corns
¼ tsp red pepper flakes
2 tsp sugar
Water

1 Tbs butter
1 onion, chopped
¼ lb. lean ham, diced
¼ lb. veal, diced
2 Tbs parsley, chopped
3 Tbs flour
1 2-lb. can Italian tomatoes,
  drained (reserve juice)

2 8-oz. bottles clam juice
Reserved shrimp broth

1 Tbs butter
½ green pepper, chopped
2 celery stalks, chopped
1 package frozen okra, thawed
  and cut into ¾" pieces
2 or 3 Tbs gumbo filé

214

SHRIMP GUMBO (*American*)

Preparation . . .

1. Assemble and prepare all ingredients.
2. Scald shrimp in seasoned boiling water just to cover; strain and reserve broth. Cool shrimp, shell and devein; reserve.

3. In 6-quart casserole, melt butter and cook onion until translucent. Add ham and veal and cook, covered, for 10 minutes. Add parsley and flour, cooking until flour browns. Add tomatoes, stirring, and cook for 5 minutes.

Cooking . . .

4. Combine clam juice and reserved shrimp broth to yield 6 cups; stir into casserole. Bring to boil; reduce heat and simmer, covered, for 1 hour. If a thinner consistency is desired, reserved tomato juice may be added.

   At this point you may stop and continue later.

5. In skillet, melt butter and cook pepper for 5 minutes. Add pepper, with celery and okra, to casserole; cook for 15 minutes. Stir in shrimp and simmer, covered, for 15 minutes longer. Stir in filé powder; serve.

SHRIMP WITH MUSHROOMS AND CURRY
(*Middle Eastern*)

Serves 6
Doubles
Refrigerates

TOTAL TIME:
about 1½ hours
(1 hour preparation,
30 minutes cooking)

You will need . . .

½ cup flour
4 tsp curry powder
2 tsp salt
½ tsp pepper
2 tsp sugar

8 Tbs butter
1 cup onion, chopped
1 cup apple, chopped

3 cups chicken broth
1⅓ cups warm milk

3 Tbs butter
2 lbs. raw shrimp,
shelled and deveined

2 Tbs butter
½ lb. mushrooms, sliced

Juice of 1 lemon

Serve with . . .
condiments for curries
rice
cucumber with
yoghurt and fresh herbs
(*Middle Eastern*)
Wine suggestions:
Vouvray,
domestic dry sauterne

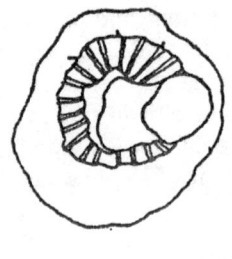

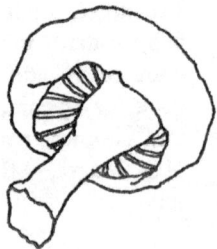

SHRIMP WITH MUSHROOMS AND CURRY
(*Middle Eastern*)

Preparation . . .

1. Assemble and prepare all ingredients.
2. Combine flour and seasonings.

3. In 6-quart casserole, melt butter and cook onion and apple until translucent.
4. Add seasoned flour to casserole, stirring to prevent lumping. Then add liquids, stirring until mixture thickens; remove from heat.

Cooking . . .

5. In skillet, melt butter, add shrimp, and cook, stirring, for 5 minutes, or until shrimp turn pink.
6. In second skillet, melt butter, add mushrooms, and cook for 5 minutes.

At this point you may stop and continue later.

7. To sauce in casserole, add shrimp and mushrooms; heat through and add lemon juice, stirring.

SHRIMP WITH SCALLOPS AND RICE–I (*Italian*)

Serves 6
Doubles
Refrigerates
Freezes

TOTAL TIME:
about 1½ hours
(1 hour preparation,
20 minutes cooking)

You will need . . .

1 lb. raw shrimp,
shelled and deveined
1 lb. sea scallops, halved
¼ cup olive oil

¼ cup olive oil
1 onion, chopped
1 clove garlic, chopped
1 green pepper, chopped
3 stalks celery, chopped
1½ cups raw natural rice

¼ tsp saffron (optional)
1 tsp turmeric
1 small can chopped pimentos
12 pitted ripe (black) olives,
quartered
4 Tbs parsley, chopped

1 7-oz. can of tuna, with oil
1 7-oz. can minced clams,
drained; reserve juice

¾ cup dry white wine
¼ cup cognac
Bottled clam juice or water

Serve with . . .
water cress and
mushroom salad
(American)
jellied sherry
(Spanish)
Wine suggestions:
domestic or imported
dry Italian white wine

Grated Parmesan cheese

SHRIMP WITH SCALLOPS AND RICE–I (*Italian*)

Preparation . . .

1. Assemble and prepare all ingredients.
2. In 6-quart casserole, combine shrimp, scallops, and oil. Cook, stirring, until shrimp begin to turn pink. Strain through colander; reserve broth.
3. In casserole, heat oil and cook onion, garlic, pepper, and celery until onion is translucent. Add rice and continue to cook, stirring, to coat with oil. Remove casserole from heat.
4. Stir in these five ingredients.

5. Add tuna and clams, and then reserved shrimp and scallops.
6. Combine shrimp-scallop broth with reserved clam juice; add wine and cognac; add bottled clam juice or water to yield 3 cups.

At this point you may stop and continue later.

Cooking . . .

7. Bring combined liquids to boil and pour over fish-rice mixture, stirring well. Bake, covered, at 350° for 20 to 30 minutes, or until rice is tender and liquid absorbed.
8. Serve with side dish of cheese.

SHRIMP WITH SCALLOPS AND RICE—II (*Middle Eastern*)

Serves 6
Doubles
Refrigerates
Freezes

TOTAL TIME:
about 1½ hours
(1 hour preparation,
30 minutes cooking)

You will need . . .

¼ cup oil
1 lb. raw shrimp,
shelled and deveined
1 lb. sea scallops, halved
1 clove garlic, minced
1 tsp salt
½ tsp cracked peppercorns
¾ tsp ground clove
¾ tsp ground ginger
¾ tsp ground cumin

1½ cups raw natural rice
3 Tbs oil

Bottled clam juice or water
Grated rind and juice of 1 lemon

Geography and flavor separate this recipe from its preceding Italian cousin.

3 bananas, quartered lengthwise

Serve with . . .
zucchini with tomatoes
(Syrian)
cucumber with yoghurt
and fresh herbs (Syrian)
Wine suggestions:
domestic or imported
dry sauterne

SHRIMP WITH SCALLOPS AND RICE—II (*Middle Eastern*)

Preparation . . .

1. Assemble and prepare all ingredients.
2. In 6-quart casserole, heat oil, add shrimp, scallops, and seasonings; cook, stirring, until shrimp starts to turn pink. Strain through colander, reserving broth.
3. In casserole, cook rice in oil, stirring, to coat each grain. Add seafood to rice, stir to blend.
4. Combine reserved broth with clam juice or water to yield 3 cups. Add lemon rind and juice.

   At this point you may stop and continue later.

5. Bring liquid to boil, add to casserole, stirring well. Cook, covered, at 350° for 20 to 30 minutes, or until rice is tender and liquid absorbed. Arrange bananas over rice for last 5 minutes of cooking.

SHRIMP, SWEET-AND-SOUR—MAISON (*Chinese*)

*Serves 6
Doubles reasonably well
Refrigerates if necessary*

TOTAL TIME:
*about 1¼ hours
(1 hour preparation,
15 minutes cooking)*

For doubling and refrigerating, see "Shrimp with Bamboo Shoots," p. 206.

This is a sort-of-Chinese recipe, devised to avoid the deep-fat frying customary with sweet-and-sour dishes.

*Serve with . . .
rice
vegetables* (Chinese)
kumquat and leechee nut compote (Chinese)
(*a good China tea, rather than wine, is the best accompaniment to Chinese food*)

You will need . . .

1½ lbs. raw shrimp,
shelled and deveined

2 Tbs sugar
1 tsp salt
3 Tbs soy sauce
6 Tbs cider vinegar
Pineapple juice,
drained from 20-oz. can
of pineapple chunks
1 tsp ground ginger

1 green pepper, coarsely chopped
1 cup sliced mushrooms
1 Tbs ginger root, chopped
(preserved will do)
1 can water chestnuts, quartered
Reserved pineapple chunks

4 Tbs oil

2 Tbs cornstarch
¼ cup water

SHRIMP, SWEET-AND-SOUR—MAISON (Chinese)

Preparation . . .

1. Assemble and prepare all ingredients.
2. In saucepan, combine these six ingredients.

3. Combine these five ingredients.

At this point you may stop and continue later.

Cooking . . .

4. Heat 6-quart casserole, add oil. Add shrimp and cook until pink.
5. Bring pineapple juice mixture to boil.
6. Add vegetable mixture to casserole. Pour boiling sauce over and cook for 5 minutes.
7. Mix cornstarch with water, add to casserole, and cook, stirring, until sauce thickens.

SHRIMP WITH VEGETABLES (*Chinese*)

Serves 6
Doubles reasonably well
Refrigerates if necessary

TOTAL TIME:
about 1¼ hours
(1 hour preparation,
15 minutes cooking)

For doubling and refrigerating, see "Shrimp with Bamboo Shoots," p. 206.

You will need . . .

1½ lbs. raw shrimp,
shelled and deveined

12 scallions, sliced
1 cup celery, coarsely chopped
1 can water chestnuts,
drained and quartered
1 can bean sprouts, drained
1 package frozen pea pods, thawed

2 Tbs soy sauce
¼ tsp salt
1 tsp ginger root, chopped
(preserved will do)
1 Tbs sherry

2 Tbs oil

2 Tbs oil

1 Tbs cornstarch
½ cup chicken broth

Serve with . . .
rice
kumquat and
leechee nut compote
(*Chinese*)
(a good China tea, rather than wine, is the best accompaniment to Chinese food)

SHRIMP WITH VEGETABLES (Chinese)

Preparation . . .

1. Assemble and prepare all ingredients.

2. Combine these five ingredients.

3. Combine these four ingredients.

At this point you may stop and continue later.

4. Dredge shrimp in soy sauce mixture.

Cooking . . .

5. Heat 6-quart casserole, add oil, and cook shrimp until pink; remove.
6. Reheat casserole, add oil, and cook vegetables for 3 minutes.
7. Meanwhile, combine cornstarch and broth. Add shrimp to casserole, pour broth mixture over, and cook, stirring, until sauce thickens.

Main Dish Soups and Soup-Stews

Soups and soup-stews are easily made. Most of them "hold" indefinitely. Not only are they satisfying, but also they simplify menu-making: a soup-stew, a breadstuff, and a salad with cheese and/or fruit constitute a full meal.

The following recipes may be made in advance; all may be refrigerated and many may be frozen. Allow refrigerated or frozen dishes to reach room temperature before reheating gently to serve.

Recipes for the suggested side dishes given with each main dish may be found elsewhere in the book.

FISH STEW WITH VEGETABLES (*French*)

Serves 6 to 8
Doubles
Refrigerates

TOTAL TIME:
about 1¾ hours
(45 minutes preparation,
1 hour cooking)

The broth from this Provençal dish may be served separately from the fish and vegetables.

Serve with . . .
bread en casserole
(French)
spinach salad (French)
and French cheese of your choice
pears with red wine
(French)
Wine suggestions:
domestic or imported
vin rosé

You will need . . .

4 medium potatoes,
peeled and cut in ⅛'s
4 medium onions, thickly sliced
4 carrots, scraped and
cut in bite-size pieces
4 stalks celery,
cut in bite-size pieces
2 green peppers,
cut in lengthwise strips
1 2-lb. can Italian tomatoes
1 4-oz. can chopped pimentos
2 or 3 cloves garlic, minced
2 bay leaves, crushed
2 Tbs dried parsley flakes
1 tsp oregano
Grated rind of 1 orange
1 Tbs sugar
2 tsp salt
½ tsp pepper
⅓ cup olive oil
Boiling water

2½ lbs. filet of cod or scrod,
cut into large bite-size pieces
Paprika
Chopped fresh parsley (optional)

FISH STEW WITH VEGETABLES (*French*)

Preparation . . .

1. Assemble and prepare all ingredients.

Cooking . . .

2. In lightly oiled 6-quart casserole, arrange all ingredients (except fish) in layers as they appear in column at left. Finish with garlic, seasonings, and oil. Pour over boiling water to level of carrots. Bring to second boil; reduce heat and simmer, covered, for 40 minutes, or until potatoes and carrots are tender.

At this point you may stop and continue later.

3. Lay fish over simmering vegetables and steam, covered, for 15 minutes, or until fish flakes easily. Garnish with paprika and parsley.

229

HAM AND BEAN SOUP WITH VEGETABLES (*French*)

Serves 6
Doubles
Refrigerates
Freezes

TOTAL TIME:
about 6 hours
(*1½ hours preparation,
4½ hours cooking*)

A hearty Basque dish welcome for winter evening suppers.

Serve with . . .
*bread en casserole
(French)
spinach salad (French)
with French cheese of your choice
peaches with red wine
(French)
Wine suggestions:
red Côtes du Rhone,
domestic claret*

You will need . . .

1 lb. dried beans, navy or pea
6 cups water

1 2-lb. (approx.) ham butt
4 onions, sliced
4 cloves garlic, chopped
1 green pepper, chopped
¼ tsp crushed red pepper
1 lb. dried fava or lima beans
4 carrots, sliced
4 turnips, sliced
Water

½ small cabbage, shredded
1 package frozen peas
2 tsp salt
½ tsp pepper

12 pork sausages
cut in ½″ pieces

HAM AND BEAN SOUP WITH VEGETABLES (*French*)

Preparation . . .

1. Assemble and prepare all ingredients.

   In 6-quart casserole or large soup kettle, combine beans with water, bring to boil, and cook vigorously for 5 minutes. Remove from heat and let stand, covered, for 1 hour. Return to heat and simmer, covered, for 1 hour, or until just tender.

Cooking . . .

2. To casserole, add these eight ingredients and water as necessary to cover. Simmer, covered, for 3½ hours.

3. Add cabbage and peas. (Here Basque cooks add any other vegetables at hand: celery, spinach, etc.) Cook, covered, for one hour, or until mixture is thick. Season with salt and pepper.

   At this point you may stop and continue later.

4. Remove ham butt; cut meat in bite-size pieces and reserve. Grill sausage until crisp. Just before serving, stir in ham and sausage bits.

ONION SOUP (*Flemish*)

Serves 6
Doubles
Refrigerates

TOTAL TIME:
about 1 hour
(40 minutes preparation,
20 minutes cooking)

These directions for onion soup gratinée differ from the standard ones in using nearly double the quantity of onions, and water instead of beef stock or bouillon. (I subscribe heartily to the number of onions suggested, but urge, for a richer soup, a combination of half bouillon, half water.)

You will need . . .

7 large onions, sliced
4 Tbs butter

2 quarts boiling water
(see notes)
1 tsp salt
¼ tsp pepper

2 Tbs flour
Water

Grated Gruyère cheese

Serve with . . .
gougère (French)
potato salad (French)
pears with red wine
(French)
or
bread en casserole
(French)
spinach salad (French)
and French cheese of your
choice
individual chocolate mousse
(French)
Wine suggestions:
red Bordeaux,
domestic claret

ONION SOUP (*Flemish*)

Preparation . . .

1. Assemble and prepare all ingredients.
2. In 6-quart casserole or soup kettle, cook onions with butter until of an even gold color.

   At this point you may stop and continue later.

3. Add liquid and seasonings.

Cooking . . .

4. Mix flour with a little water, stirring until smooth; add to soup. Boil soup, gently, for 20 minutes.
5. Serve cheese separately.

PEA SOUP (*Dutch*)

Serves 6
Doubles
Refrigerates
Freezes

TOTAL TIME:
(*45 minutes preparation,
3½ hours cooking*)

The Erwtensoep of Holland differs from American split-pea soup because of its smoky frankfurter taste.

Serve with . . .
*bock beer bread
(German)
salad with dressing
and Edam cheese
jellied sherry (Spanish)
Wine suggestions:
domestic or imported
red Burgundy*

You will need . . .

3 qts. water
4 cups split green peas
1½ tsp salt
1 tsp sugar
2 pig's feet

½ lb. bacon, diced

3 leeks, washed and sliced
(8 scallions will do)
3 onions, chopped
1½ cups celery, chopped, with tops

4 Tbs parsley, chopped

6 to 8 frankfurters, cut in ¼" slices
and browned in butter

PEA SOUP (*Dutch*)

Preparation . . .

1. Assemble and prepare all ingredients.

Cooking . . .

2. In 6-quart casserole or soup kettle, combine water, peas, and seasonings. Bring to boil. Add pig's feet and simmer, covered, for 2 hours.

   In skillet, render bacon; drain on absorbent paper and reserve. Reserve 3 Tbs of fat.
3. In reserved fat, cook leeks, onions, and celery until onions are translucent; add to casserole.

   At this point you may stop and continue later.
4. Add parsley and reserved bacon.
5. Continue to simmer, covered, for 1½ hours, or until pig's feet are tender. Remove pig's feet; discard skin and bone; reserve meat.
6. To casserole, add meat from pig's feet and frankfurter slices.

   May be garnished with croutons, if desired.

   For Danish pea soup, add 3 carrots, thinly sliced, when cooking vegetables in bacon fat.

POTATO SOUP *(French)*

Serves 6
Doubles
Refrigerates

TOTAL TIME:
about 3 hours
(1 hour preparation
2 hours cooking)

Potage parmentier, *potato soup, is named for the man who popularized potatoes in France.*

Serve with . . .
muffins (American)
Caesar salad (American)
pears with curry
(Middle Eastern)
Wine suggestions:
white Burgundy,
domestic dry sauterne

You will need . . .

1 lb. potatoes, peeled and diced
2 leeks, washed and sliced
(6 scallions will do)
2 onions, sliced
2 carrots, sliced
2 stalks celery, with tops, chopped
Several sprigs parsley
1 tsp salt
¼ tsp pepper
1 tsp sugar
2½ qts. water

4 Tbs butter
½ cup heavy cream

POTATO SOUP (*French*)

Preparation . . .

1. Assemble and prepare all ingredients.

Cooking . . .

2. In 6-quart casserole or soup kettle, combine these ten ingredients and bring to boil; reduce heat and simmer, covered, for 2 hours.

3. Drain vegetables; reserve liquid. Put vegetables through sieve. Return vegetable pulp and liquid to casserole.

    At this point you may stop and continue later.

4. To simmering casserole, add butter and cream; adjust seasoning.

    For a richer soup, use 1 qt. chicken broth and 1½ qts. water; increase amount of cream, to taste.

VEGETABLE SOUP WITH MEAT (*Afghanistan*)

*Serves 6
Doubles
Refrigerates*

TOTAL TIME:
*about 2 hours
(45 minutes preparation,
1¼ hours cooking)*

You will need . . .

4 Tbs butter
1½ lbs. ground round

2 onions, chopped
1 clove garlic, chopped
1 green pepper, chopped
1 1-lb. can Italian tomatoes
1 tsp salt
1 tsp sugar
Pinch cayenne
1 cup water

½ lb. noodles
1 qt. boiling salted water
2 cups canned kidney beans, drained
2 cups yoghurt

Dried mint flakes

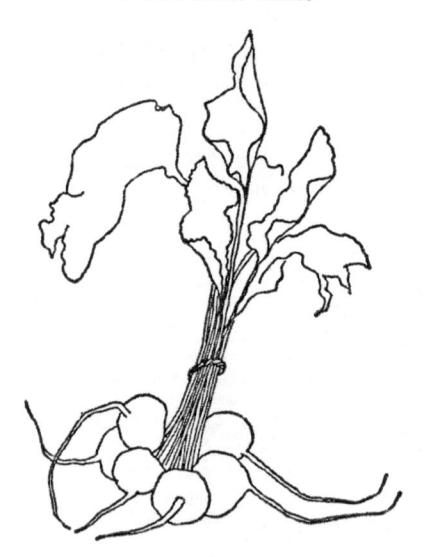

*Serve with . . .
muffins (American)
cucumbers with orange
and green pepper
(Middle Eastern)
Wine suggestions:
red Bordeaux,
domestic claret*

VEGETABLE SOUP WITH MEAT (*Afghanistan*)

Preparation . . .

1. Assemble and prepare all ingredients.
2. In 6-quart casserole or soup kettle, melt butter and brown meat.

Cooking . . .

3. Add these eight ingredients and cook, covered, at 325° for 1 hour. Remove from heat; stir.

At this point you may stop and continue later.

4. Cook noodles in water for 10 minutes; do not drain. To noodles, add kidney beans and heat through. Remove from heat and stir in yoghurt. Add noodle mixture to casserole and mix well.
5. When serving, garnish with mint.

FISH CHOWDER (*American*)

Serves 6
Doubles
Refrigerates

TOTAL TIME:
about 1½ hours
(45 minutes preparation,
45 minutes cooking)

You will need . . .

¼ lb. salt pork, diced
4 onions, chopped
2 carrots, thinly sliced
4 stalks celery, chopped
2 cups raw potato, finely diced

1 Tbs butter
1½ Tbs flour
1 cup clam juice

1½ lbs. cod filet,
cut in bite-size pieces
1½ lbs. haddock filet,
cut in bite-size pieces
1 qt. whole milk
1 cup heavy cream

Salt
Pepper
Pinch of cayenne
½ cup sherry

Serve with . . .
bread en casserole,
Variation I or II
(American)
spinach salad with orange
and bacon (American)
Wine suggestions:
white Burgundy,
domestic dry sauterne

FISH CHOWDER (*American*)

Preparation . . .

1. Assemble and prepare all ingredients.

Cooking . . .

2. In 6-quart casserole or soup kettle, render salt pork, until crisp and golden; remove and reserve. Add onions and cook until translucent. Add carrots and celery and cook, stirring, until well coated with fat. Add potatoes and repeat.
3. In saucepan, melt butter and add flour, stirring; add clam juice and cook, stirring, until mixture thickens. Add to casserole and cook, covered, for 10 minutes, or until potato is tender.

   At this point you may stop and continue later.

4. Add fish to casserole. Combine milk and cream, scald, and pour boiling over fish; simmer, covered, for 10 minutes.

5. Adjust seasoning. Just before serving, stir in sherry.

   Carrots, celery, and sherry—one or all—may be omitted. If desired, ¾ cup finely chopped fresh parsley may be added at serving.

   1 tsp curry powder may be added to the butter and flour before clam juice is stirred in.

FISH CHOWDER WITH PINEAPPLE (*Cambodian*)

*Serves 6
Doubles
Refrigerates*

TOTAL TIME:
*about 1 hour
(45 minutes preparation,
15 minutes cooking)*

You will need . . .

4 Tbs oil
2 cloves garlic, minced
2 onions, chopped
6 cups water
⅓ cup sherry
Grated rind and juice of 1 orange
2 bay leaves, broken
½ tsp dried crushed red pepper flakes
¾ tsp cumin seed
¼ tsp saffron
1 20-oz. can crushed pineapple,
with juice

2 lbs. cod filet,
cut in bite-size pieces
1 lb. raw shrimp,
shelled and deveined

2 Tbs soy sauce
3 Tbs cornstarch

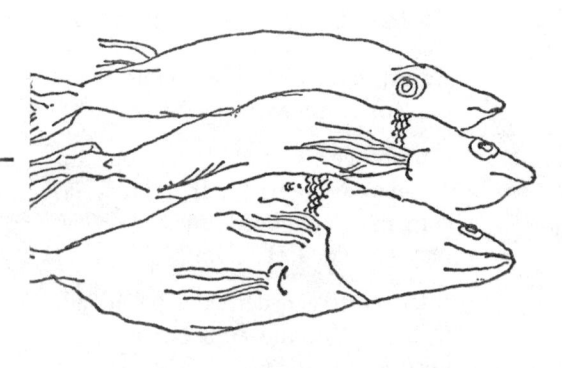

*Serve with . . .
bulgur salad
(Middle Eastern)
peaches with curry
(Middle Eastern)
Wine suggestions:
white Côtes du Rhone,
domestic Chablis*

242

FISH CHOWDER WITH PINEAPPLE (*Cambodian*)

Preparation . . .

1. Assemble and prepare all ingredients.
2. In 6-quart casserole or soup kettle, heat oil; cook garlic and onion until translucent. Add water, sherry, orange rind and juice, seasonings, and pineapple with juice. Bring to boil and simmer, covered, for 30 minutes.

At this point you may stop and continue later.

Cooking . . .

3. To simmering casserole, add fish and shrimp; cook, covered, for 10 minutes.

4. Mix soy sauce and cornstarch; add to casserole, stirring gently, until soup thickens.

   If desired, this dish may be served over boiled rice.

SCALLOP STEW (*American*)

Serves 6
Doubles
Refrigerates

TOTAL TIME:
about 1 hour
(30 minutes preparation,
30 minutes cooking)

A dish from Montauk, Long Island, New York, where the preparation of such food is traditionally expert.

Serve with . . .
oatmeal-raisin bread
(American)
wilted lettuce salad
(American)
dried fruit compote
Wine suggestions:
Neuchâtel,
domestic Chablis

You will need . . .

2 potatoes, peeled and diced
2 onions, chopped
3 stalks celery, chopped
Water

1½ lbs. sea scallops, halved
1 qt. milk
1 cup heavy cream
¾ tsp salt
¼ tsp white pepper
Dash Tabasco
Chopped fresh parsley, to taste
Butter, to taste

SCALLOP STEW (*American*)

Preparation . . .

1. Assemble and prepare all ingredients.

Cooking . . .

2. In 6-quart casserole or soup kettle, combine potatoes, onions, and celery with water just to cover. Bring to boil; reduce heat and simmer, covered, for 20 minutes, or until potatoes are tender.

   At this point you may stop and continue later.

3. Add scallops to casserole. Combine milk and cream, scald, and pour over scallops. Simmer gently for 10 minutes; do not allow to boil. Add seasonings and parsley, stirring gently. Just before serving, add butter.

SEAFOOD STEW—MAISON (*American*)

Serves 6
Doubles
Refrigerates

TOTAL TIME:
about 45 minutes
(30 minutes preparation,
15 minutes cooking)

You will need . . .

1 8-oz. can lobster meat
2 8-oz. cans crab meat

¾ lb. raw shrimp,
shelled and deveined
12 oysters, with juice
4 Tbs butter

1 can minced clams
1 can frozen shrimp soup,
thawed and undiluted
1 tsp Worcestershire sauce
3 cups whole milk
1 cup heavy cream
Salt
Pepper
Paprika

¼ cup sherry

Serve with . . .
muffins (American)
salad with dressing
gingerbread (American)
or
blueberry duff (American)
Wine suggestions:
domestic or imported
vin rosé

SEAFOOD STEW—MAISON (*American*)

Preparation . . .

1. Assemble and prepare all ingredients.
2. Pick over lobster and crab meat, removing tendons.

Cooking . . .

3. In 6-quart casserole or soup kettle, combine lobster, crab, shrimp, oysters with juice, and butter. Cook gently, stirring, for 5 minutes.
4. To casserole, add clams with juice, shrimp soup, and Worcestershire sauce. Combine milk and cream, scald, and pour over all. Simmer gently for 10 minutes; do not allow to boil. Season to taste.

5. When serving, add sherry.

Part Two
A FEW COMPANIONABLE SIDE DISHES

Rice, Barley, and Bulgur

Rice, barley, and bulgur are the most healthful and least fattening of the starches. Rice is in such general use that for menu-making it claims no particular nationality; barley and bulgur (cracked wheat) are primarily Middle Eastern. All three go well with virtually every main dish in this book. They are prepared in similar ways. They lend themselves to various seasonings, from bland to hot-and-spicy. They give weight to a meal without making the eater feel heavy. They are more satisfactory, I feel, than spaghetti or noodles, for they absorb the liquid in which they are cooked and require no last-minute draining, rinsing, or buttering.

Refrigerating and freezing rice, barley, and bulgur, once cooked, may be done successfully (for this, the casserole method of cooking is best, p. 252). The dish must reach room temperature before reheating—gently, to prevent the grains from going mushy. Refrigerating barley or bulgur is more successful than refrigerating or freezing rice—perhaps because there is more "body" to their grain.

One digression on rice: I avoid pre-cooked varieties. Boiling natural rice requires, from start to finish, only twenty-five minutes, during which time you can do other things. The results with natural rice, compared with those of speed-cooking brands, are both more flavorful and consistent.

BOILED RICE, BARLEY, or BULGUR

Serves 6
Doubles
Refrigerates
Freezes

TOTAL TIME:
about 25 minutes

You will need . . .

2 Tbs oil or butter
1½ cups rice, barley, or bulgur

3 cups water
¾ tsp salt

RICE, BARLEY, or BULGUR EN CASSEROLE

Serves 6
Doubles
Refrigerates
Freezes

TOTAL TIME:
about 25 minutes (rice);
see other times below

You will need . . .

2 Tbs oil or butter
1½ cups rice, barley, or bulgur

3 cups boiling water
¾ tsp salt

BOILED RICE, BARLEY or BULGUR

Preparation and cooking . . .

1. In heavy saucepan with tight-fitting lid, heat oil or butter. Add rice, barley, or bulgur and cook, stirring with fork until each grain is coated.
2. Add water and salt, bring to boil, and stir once with fork; reduce heat and simmer, covered, for 15 minutes, or until grains are tender and liquid is absorbed.

Allow approximately 25 minutes for barley.

RICE, BARLEY, or BULGUR EN CASSEROLE

Preparation and cooking . . .

1. In saucepan, heat oil or butter. Add rice, barley, or bulgur and cook, stirring with fork until each grain is coated. Transfer grain to casserole.

   The use of flame-proof casserole eliminates need of saucepan.
2. Add water and salt, stir once with fork; bake, covered, at 350° for . . .

   18 to 25 minutes for rice . . .

   45 to 50 minutes for barley and bulgur . . .

   or until grains are tender and liquid is absorbed.

   Barley *en casserole* may be given an extra fillip by stirring in ½ cup yoghurt just before serving.

RICE, BARLEY, or BULGUR

Rice, barley, and bulgur derive their particular flavors from the liquids in which they are cooked, as well as from seasonings. The following liquids, at full strength or diluted, may be used instead of water:

>chicken or beef broth or bouillon
>consommé
>left-over clear soup or home-made stock
>clam juice

Before adding the liquid, you may season the grain with one or more of the following (suggested quantities are for 1½ cups grain, or 6 servings):

- 1 tsp ground allspice
- ½ tsp dried basil
- 1 or 2 bay leaves, broken
- ½ tsp dried chervil
- 1 tsp curry powder
- ½ tsp dried dill weed
- ½ tsp dried marjoram
- 1 or 2 Tbs minced onion
- ½ tsp dried rosemary, crumbled
- ¼ tsp saffron, powdered
- ½ tsp dried sage
- ½ tsp dried thyme
- ¾ tsp turmeric
- ¼ cup dried currants or seedless raisins

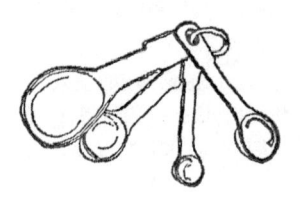

RICE, BARLEY, or BULGUR

For further flavor, as well as for visual appeal, you may stir in at serving time:

- 6 or 8 mushrooms, sliced and sautéed
- 2 or 3 Tbs dried or freshly chopped parsley
- 2 or 3 Tbs pine nuts or slivered almonds
- 3 scallions, fincly chopped (including green tops)
- 1 small can chopped pimentos

In addition to these possibilities for rice, barley, and bulgur, following are three particular rice recipes:

RICE WITH ORANGE AND THYME—MAISON (*American*)

Serves 6
Doubles
Refrigerates

TOTAL TIME:
about 30 minutes

Prepare rice in usual way, using as cooking liquid equal parts of
water
orange juice

seasoned with

grated rind of 1 orange
½ tsp thyme
¾ tsp salt

RICE WITH SAFFRON AND TOMATOES (*Spanish*)

Serves 6
Doubles
Refrigerates

TOTAL TIME:
about 35 minutes

You will need . . .

3 Tbs bacon fat
(3 slices, rendered)
1 cup natural rice

2 cloves garlic, pressed
2 small onions, minced
1 green pepper, minced
3 tomatoes, peeled and diced

2 cups beef bouillon
¼ tsp saffron, powdered

BROWN RICE WITH CURRANTS AND SCALLIONS (*American*)

Serves 6
Doubles
Refrigerates
Freezes

TOTAL TIME:
about 50 minutes

You will need . . .

1½ cups brown rice
3 cups chicken broth
1 tsp turmeric

¼ cup dried currants
6 to 8 scallions, finely chopped
(green tops, too)
2 tsp preserved ginger, minced
3 Tbs soft butter

Brown or unpolished rice has a firmer texture than white; its flavor is distinctive, quite different from that of its more refined relative.

RICE WITH SAFFRON AND TOMATOES (*Spanish*)

Preparation and cooking . . .

1. In saucepan with tight-fitting lid, melt fat. Add rice and cook, stirring with fork until each grain is coated.
2. Make space in center of rice; add garlic and cook briefly; mix with rice. Repeat with onions, then pepper, then tomatoes.
3. Add bouillon and saffron, bring to boil and stir once with fork; reduce heat and simmer, covered, for 15 minutes, or until rice is tender and liquid absorbed. If desired, garnish with reserved bacon, crumbled.

BROWN RICE WITH CURRANTS AND SCALLIONS (*American*)

Preparation and cooking . . .

1. In heavy saucepan with tight-fitting lid, combine rice, broth, and turmeric, and bring to boil; reduce heat and simmer, covered, for 45 minutes, or until rice is tender and liquid absorbed.
2. Using two forks (to keep grains separated), toss rice with currants, scallions, ginger, and butter. Let stand, covered, for a few minutes before serving.

If desired, this recipe may be cooked in casserole (see p. 252); add currants, scallions, ginger, and butter after cooking.

Despite my personal preference for rice, barley, and bulgur, several main-dish recipes are traditionally served with noodles or spaghetti—veal with paprika, beef with beer and herbs, goulash. A successful method of cooking noodles or spaghetti, and one which prevents their sticking to the kettle, is to bring the necessary quantity of salted water to boil, add the pasta, and remove from heat; allow to stand, covered, for 20 minutes without stirring; drain.

Vegetables

The following two ways of cooking frozen green vegetables are flavor- and texture-preserving, and less trouble than the usual method. The vegetable, placed in heavy saucepan or oven casserole, cooks with no added water and stays crisp and fresh.

Method I—Put the frozen block or blocks in heavy saucepan with tight-fitting lid. Dot with 1 or 2 Tbs butter for each block. Place over high heat until steam rises; at once reduce heat and simmer, covered, for 25 to 30 minutes. When vegetable is thawed, turn once with fork to distribute liquid and butter. Salt vegetable after cooking.

If you are planning *fresh* green vegetables, a variation of Method I works well: prepare and wash as usual, allowing water to cling to the vegetable; proceed as in Method I.

Method II—Put frozen block or blocks in casserole. Dot with 1 or 2 Tbs butter for each block. Cook in oven, covered, at 350° for 45 minutes, or until vegetable is tender (timings are for *al dente*, crisp, greens). When vegetable is thawed, turn once with fork to distribute liquid and butter. Salt vegetable after cooking.

Lima beans and peas may be prepared by Method II: add ¼ cup water for each package of vegetable.

Method II will *not* work for fresh green vegetables.

Neither Method I nor II is applicable to frozen *starchy* vegetables—for which, follow directions on package.

Salt tends to wilt vegetables; therefore use it after cooking.

Vegetables

A little sugar, however, sprinkled on at cooking time, does not destroy vegetable tissue and, like salt, brings out natural flavor.

Green vegetables may be seasoned in cooking with:

½ tsp herb of your choice
(see "Rice, Barley, and Bulgur," p. 254
—the same herbs work well with vegetables)
a sprinkling of grated cheese
chopped chives
a sprinkling of lemon juice
poppy seed
chopped scallions
and/or
a packet of powdered chicken broth sprinkled over

Of the following recipes, only Mixed Vegetables In Casserole, p. 260 and Ratatouille, p. 262, will freeze successfully; and they must reach room temperature before being gently reheated. The other recipes may be refrigerated but it should be remembered that vegetables, once cooked and refrigerated, change in texture and sometimes in taste. The following dishes and their variations may often be prepared in advance of cooking time. The first three recipes for mixed vegetable casseroles follow the format of the main dishes in Part I; the recipes for simpler vegetable courses are given in simpler format.

MIXED VEGETABLES EN CASSEROLE (*Rumanian*)

Serves 6
Doubles
Refrigerates
Freezes

TOTAL TIME:
about 50 minutes
(*20 minutes preparation,*
30 minutes cooking)

Excepting the eggplant and cabbage, this dish may be made with frozen foods. It also serves as a main course for suppers.

You will need . . .

¼ cup olive oil
3 onions, chopped

1 package frozen sliced carrots
1 package frozen lima beans
1 package frozen green beans
1 package frozen cauliflower
¼ cup frozen chopped green pepper
1 small eggplant, peeled and diced
6 scallions, chopped, with as much green as possible
½ small cabbage, shredded
2 cloves garlic, chopped
4 Tbs dried parsley flakes
½ tsp thyme
½ tsp marjoram
¼ tsp rosemary
½ tsp savory
2 tsp sugar
1 tsp salt
¼ tsp pepper

1 1-lb. can Italian tomatoes

½ cup oil (a mixture of olive and corn oils)
½ cup bouillon

MIXED VEGETABLES EN CASSEROLE (*Rumanian*)

Preparation . . .

1. Assemble and prepare all ingredients.
   Frozen vegetables should be thawed to allow tossing them.
2. In lightly greased 6-quart casserole, heat oil; cook onion until translucent; remove and reserve.
3. In casserole, toss together vegetables, herbs, and seasonings.

At this point you may stop and continue later.

4. Fold in reserved onion and tomatoes.

Cooking . . .

5. Combine oil and bouillon, bring to boil, and pour over contents of casserole. Bake, covered, at 350° for 30 minutes, or until vegetables are tender and liquid is absorbed. To dry dish further, remove cover and continue cooking a few minutes, stirring once.

RATATOUILLE (French)

Serves 6
Doubles
Refrigerates
Freezes

TOTAL TIME:
about 1¾ hours
(30 minutes preparation,
1¼ hours cooking)

This vegetable stew of Provençal origin may be served either hot or cold. It is sometimes listed on restaurant menus as "ratatouille niçoise," commemorating that sunny city overlooking the Mediterranean.

You will need . . .

¼ cup olive oil
2 cloves garlic, chopped
2 onions, chopped

1 large eggplant, cut in 1″ cubes
Flour
1 green pepper,
cut in julienne strips

3 zucchini, cut in ½″ pieces
4 tomatoes, peeled and quartered
1 tsp salt
¼ tsp pepper
2 tsp sugar
1 tsp dried oregano

RATATOUILLE (French)

Preparation . . .

1. Assemble and prepare all ingredients.
2. In 6-quart casserole, heat oil; cook garlic and onions until translucent.

Cooking . . .

3. Dredge eggplant in flour and add to casserole with pepper; simmer, covered, over lowest possible heat for 1 hour. Add a little water, if necessary.

   At this point you may stop and continue later.

4. Add zucchini, tomatoes, and seasonings; simmer, covered, for 15 minutes. Stir to blend well. If mixture is too liquid, remove cover and simmer a few minutes longer; ratatouille should be moist but not liquid.

SWEET-AND-SOUR VEGETABLES–MAISON (*Chinese*)

Serves 6
Doubles
Refrigerates

TOTAL TIME:
*about 40 minutes
(30 minutes preparation,
10 minutes cooking)*

For doubling and refrigerating, see "Shrimp with Bamboo Shoots," p. 206.

You will need . . .

1 head celery cabbage
(or 4 endive), cut in ¾"
slices, washed and drained
1 green pepper, chopped
1 package frozen pea pods, thawed
6 scallions, chopped
1 can bean sprouts, drained
1 can water chestnuts,
drained and sliced
(sliced radishes will do)
1 can bamboo shoots, drained
¾ lb. mushrooms, washed and sliced

2 Tbs sugar
1 tsp salt
3 Tbs soy sauce
3 Tbs vinegar
½ cup pineapple juice, reserved
from 20-oz. can pineapple tidbits
1 tsp powdered ginger

4 Tbs oil

Reserved pineapple tidbits
3 Tbs cornstarch mixed with
¼ cup water

SWEET-AND-SOUR VEGETABLES—MAISON (*Chinese*)

Preparation . . .

1. Assemble and prepare all ingredients.

2. In saucepan, combine these six ingredients; heat until sugar is melted. Reserve.

   At this point you may stop and continue later.

Cooking . . .

3. Heat 6-quart casserole, add oil and then cabbage and pepper, cooking for 2 minutes. Add pea pods and cook for 2 minutes. Add remaining vegetables and cook for 2 minutes.
4. Add pineapple tidbits, reserved soy sauce mixture, and cornstarch; cook, stirring gently, until sauce thickens.

   A savory sauce for the same vegetables: omit the pineapple, mix 3 Tbs cornstarch with 6 Tbs soy sauce and ¼ cup each sherry and water.

GREEN BEANS WITH SOUR CREAM—MAISON (*American*)

Serves 6
Doubles
Refrigerates

TOTAL TIME:
about 45 minutes

You will need . . .

2 packages frozen green beans

½ cup parsley, chopped
½ clove garlic, minced
¾ tsp salt
¼ tsp pepper
1 cup sour cream

BRAISED ENDIVE (*French*)

Serves 6
Doubles
Refrigerates

TOTAL TIME:
about 50 minutes

You will need . . .

12 endives, washed and trimmed
Juice of ½ lemon
Butter
½ cup boiling chicken broth
Salt
Pepper

GREEN BEANS WITH SOUR CREAM—MAISON (*American*)

Preparation and cooking . . .

1. Cook beans by Method II, p. 258.
2. Gently toss cooked beans with these five ingredients; return, uncovered, to 350° oven for 10 minutes, or until heated through.

The dish may be made with 1½ lbs. fresh green beans, stemmed, rinsed, and cooked by Method I, p. 258.

If desired, 1 tsp dried dill may be added. Or 1 can of sliced mushrooms. Or both.

BRAISED ENDIVE (*French*)

Preparation and cooking . . .

In buttered baking dish, arrange endives; sprinkle with lemon juice and dot with butter. Pour over chicken broth and cook, covered, at 350° for 35 minutes, or until tender. Season with salt and pepper.

The recipe works well for fennel: allow ½ large fennel cluster per serving; cooking time is about 45 minutes.

For variation in flavor, use half-and-half chicken broth and sherry.

CARROTS WITH NUTMEG AND HONEY (*Flemish*)

Serves 6
Doubles
Refrigerates

TOTAL TIME:
about 1¼ hours

You will need . . .

12 good-sized carrots,
scraped and cut in julienne strips
(or sliced as thinly as possible)
⅓ cup honey
⅓ cup water
3 Tbs butter
Freshly grated nutmeg
¼ tsp salt

I found this dish at a restaurant in Bruges, Belgium. The variations are mine.

The dish lends itself to several variations in flavor; method of cooking remains the same:

1. Use maple syrup or old-fashioned dark brown sugar (omit honey).
2. Use orange juice (omit water).
3. Use grated rind of 1 orange in addition to nutmeg.
4. Use sprinkling of powdered ginger (omit nutmeg).
5. For a savory sauce, use ⅓ cup soy sauce instead of honey and sprinkling of powdered ginger instead of nutmeg.

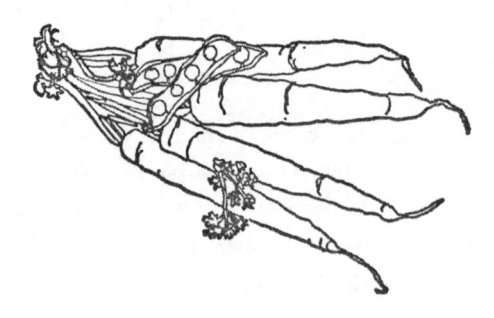

CARROTS WITH NUTMEG AND HONEY (*Flemish*)

Preparation and cooking . . .

1. In lightly buttered baking dish, arrange carrots. Mix together honey and water; pour over carrots. Dot with butter and sprinkle generously with nutmeg; add salt.

   At this point you may stop and continue later.

2. Bake, tightly covered, at 350° for 50 minutes, or until carrots are tender.

   Frozen baby carrots may be substituted for fresh ones; cooking time is reduced to about 30 minutes.

   Recipe may be prepared on top of stove in heavy skillet or saucepan with tight-fitting lid over lowest possible heat.

ONIONS WITH HONEY (*Flemish*)

Serves 6
Doubles
Refrigerates

TOTAL TIME:
about 1¼ hours

You will need...

18 small onions, peeled
Water
Salt

¾ cup honey
6 Tbs butter
Ground clove

A French recipe for onions: prepare onions as directed, reserving onion water. In buttered 2-quart casserole, arrange alternate layers of apples (peeled, cored, and sliced) and onions. Season each layer with ground cinnamon, salt, and pepper, and dot with butter. Pour over 1 cup reserved onion water. Bake as directed, or until apples are just tender.

SPINACH WITH SOUR CREAM AND HORSERADISH–MAISON (*American*)

Serves 6
Doubles
Refrigerates

TOTAL TIME:
about 35 minutes

You will need...

2 packages frozen chopped spinach

Salt
Pepper
Sour cream at room temperature
1 tsp prepared horseradish
(or more, to taste)

ONIONS WITH HONEY (*Flemish*)

Preparation and cooking . . .

1. Boil onions until just tender in slightly salted water to cover. Drain and arrange in lightly buttered baking dish.
2. Heat together honey and butter, pour over onions; sprinkle lightly with clove.

   At this point you may stop and continue later.

3. Bake onions, uncovered, at 350° for 30 minutes, or until they are golden.

SPINACH WITH SOUR CREAM AND HORSERADISH–MAISON (*American*)

Preparation and cooking . . .

1. Cook spinach by either Method I or II, p. 258.
2. Season with salt and pepper. Stir in sufficient sour cream to give desired consistency; add horseradish and blend.

A packet of powdered chicken broth may be sprinkled over spinach at time of cooking. Omit horseradish, but use sour cream.

A generous sprinkling of nutmeg (preferably freshly grated) may be used in place of horseradish.

ZUCCHINI WITH TOMATOES (*Syrian*)

Serves 6
Doubles
Refrigerates
TOTAL TIME: *about 45 minutes*

You will need . . .

4 Tbs butter or olive oil
1 onion, chopped
1½ tsp turmeric
6 to 8 zucchini, washed and cut in ½″ slices
¾ tsp salt
¼ tsp pepper
3 tomatoes, peeled and chopped
¾ tsp dried tarragon

THREE SAUCES FOR VEGETABLES

Use these sauces with vegetables prepared by either Method I or II without additional seasonings and *without butter.*

Curry Butter

In saucepan, melt 4 Tbs butter and add 1 tsp lemon juice, ¾ to 1 tsp curry powder, and ¼ tsp salt; cook until bubbly and pour over vegetable.

ZUCCHINI WITH TOMATOES (*Syrian*)

Preparation and cooking . . .

1. Prepare and ready all ingredients.
2. In skillet or flame-proof baking dish, heat butter and cook onion until translucent. Add turmeric and zucchini, stirring; cook for 5 minutes. Add remaining ingredients and cook, covered, until squash is crisp-tender (about 8 minutes for open-flame cooking, about 20 minutes for oven-baking at 350°).

Curry powder, to taste, may be used (omit turmeric).

THREE SAUCES FOR VEGETABLES

Hollandaise Sauce
In *warm* container of electric blender, put 3 egg yolks, 1 Tbs lemon juice, ¼ tsp dry mustard, and a pinch of salt. In saucepan, melt ¼ lb. of butter and bring to foaming boil. With blender running at low speed, add butter in steady, slow stream. When butter is poured, turn off blender. Place container in warm water until sauce is served.

Short-order "Hollandaise"
In saucepan, melt 4 Tbs butter; add 1 Tbs lemon juice and 5 Tbs mayonnaise (1 Tbs at a time), stirring. If sauce seems to curdle, add more mayonnaise.

A Few Salads

Before experience taught otherwise, I always assumed that salad must be prepared only at the last minute—the *whole* salad, that is, from greens to dressing to final tossing. Salad should not, indeed, be tossed with its dressing until just at serving time, but most salad greens and vegetables, if properly protected from air and refrigerated, may be readied in advance. Many salad dressings, too, may be wholly or partially prepared. Producing an appetizing salad *is* possible without rush or last-minute effort.

SALADS

Following is a list of greens which work well in almost any combination:

>Chinese or celery cabbage
>endive
>escarole
>lettuce (all varieties)
>romaine
>rugola
>spinach
>water cress

To one or a combination of these greens, you may add one or more of the following:

>artichoke hearts
>avocado pear*
>canned bamboo shoots
>raw broccoli stalks, peeled and sliced
>cherry tomatoes, halved
>cucumber, sliced
>green pepper in julienne strips
>raw sliced mushrooms
>radishes, sliced
>scallions, sliced *lengthwise*
>red onion, sliced
>canned water chestnuts, sliced

*Avocado will darken once peeled and sliced; this *is* a last-minute ingredient.

SALADS

Among favorite salad herbs and garnishes are:

> basil   oregano
> chervil   parsley
> chive   savory
> dill   tarragon
> marjoram
>
> and/or
> croutons
> hard-boiled egg
> (put through a sieve)

Although these are only partial lists, the possible combinations are numberless—and so, too, are the pleasures of discovering them.

The three salad dressings which follow are excellent "make-aheads": "all-purpose" dressing, mayonnaise, and slightly-sweet dressing for mild-flavored greens.

"ALL-PURPOSE" DRESSING—MAISON

About 1 cup
Doubles
Refrigerates
TIME: 15 minutes

You will need . . .

2 tsp sugar
1 tsp salt
½ tsp white pepper
½ tsp dry mustard (optional)
¼ cup wine vinegar or lemon juice

¾ cup oil

This dressing is a bland mixture—purposely so, for the salad may be given individuality by the use of herbs, or of a particular ingredient (such as rugola), or by adding to the dressing a clove of garlic, pressed, or ⅓ cup blue cheese, crumbled, etc.

I suggest using ½ olive and ½ corn oils; olive oil alone sometimes makes salads "heavy." This dressing, like most others, is more flavorful if used at room temperature over chilled greens.

SLIGHTLY-SWEET DRESSING (*American*)

About ½ cup
Doubles
Refrigerates
TIME: 15 minutes

You will need . . .

¼ cup honey
¼ cup oil
Juice of 1 lemon
Dash of bitters
¼ tsp salt
¼ tsp white pepper

Lemon juice gives the dressing piquancy. Use on mild-flavored greens.

"ALL-PURPOSE" DRESSING—MAISON

Preparation . . .

1. In jar with tight-fitting lid, combine sugar, salt, pepper, mustard, water, and vinegar. Shake until sugar and salt are dissolved.
2. Add oil and shake until thoroughly blended.

SLIGHTLY-SWEET DRESSING (*American*)

Preparation . . .

In jar with tight-fitting lid, combine all ingredients and shake until thoroughly blended.

If desired, a sliver of garlic may be added to marinate in dressing for 1 hour.

MAYONNAISE (*French*)

About 1¼ cups
Refrigerates

TIME:
15 minutes

You will need . . .

1 egg
½ tsp dry mustard
½ tsp salt
2 Tbs vinegar or lemon juice
¼ cup oil
(olive or corn or half-and-half)
(2 or 3 drops yellow vegetable food coloring)

¾ cup oil

I cheer the electric blender every time I make "guaranteed" hollandaise (see "Vegetables," p. 273), and every time I prepare mayonnaise, a dressing suitable for salads, hors d'oeuvres, many vegetables, cold meats, and fish.

MAYONNAISE (*French*)

Preparation . . .

1. Put these six ingredients in container of electric blender; cover and turn to low speed.
2. Immediately uncover and add remaining oil in slow, steady stream. If necessary, stop blender and, with rubber spatula, push ingredients into path of blades. When oil is blended, stop machine.

Garlic mayonnaise, *aioli*, traditionally made in a marble mortar, may also be prepared in the blender: add, with the first six ingredients for mayonnaise, 1 or 2 cloves of garlic, minced.

Green mayonnaise, the *real*, not just colored, calls for a different, but equally easy procedure; its uses are the same as for ordinary mayonnaise. Directions for preparing it are found on p. 324.

CAESAR SALAD (*American*)

Serves 6
Doubles
TIME:
30 minutes

You will need . . .

2 large heads romaine,
cut in 1" "slices,"
well washed and drained
Juice of 1 lemon
1 egg, raw or coddled
Generous sprinkling oregano

½ tsp salt
Fresh-ground pepper, to taste
1 can flat anchovy filets,
separated and cut in 1" lengths
OR
6 to 8 strips bacon,
rendered crisp and crumbled

A summertime supper by itself and at any time a substantial salad. The romaine may be prepared ahead of time and refrigerated; so may the dressing, if you make it in a blender (see below). Serve the salad, however, as soon as it is tossed.

¼ cup oil
1 clove garlic, pressed

4 Tbs grated cheese

½ cup bread croutons

CUCUMBERS WITH ORANGES AND SOUR CREAM (*Middle Eastern*)

Serves 6
Doubles
Refrigerates
TIME:
about 45 minutes

You will need . . .

1 cup sour cream
2 Tbs fresh mint, chopped
1 tsp sugar
½ tsp salt

3 or 4 oranges,
peeled, seeded, thinly sliced
3 or 4 cucumbers,
peeled, quartered lengthwise,
cut in 1" pieces

This salad serves well as dessert.

CAESAR SALAD (*American*)

Preparation . . .

1. In large salad bowl, combine first three ingredients; toss thoroughly.
2. Add salt and pepper and anchovies (or bacon); toss thoroughly.
3. Mix oil and garlic and add to salad; toss thoroughly.
4. Add cheese; toss thoroughly.
5. Sprinkle croutons on top; serve.

Lemon juice, egg, oregano, salt, pepper, oil, garlic, and cheese may be combined in container of electric blender (at low speed for 15 seconds); if you use anchovies, add them, too, together with oil in which they are packed.

CUCUMBERS WITH ORANGES AND SOUR CREAM
(*Middle Eastern*)

Preparation . . .

1. Combine these four ingredients to make dressing.
2. Combine oranges and cucumber with dressing; mix well. Chill.

This salad may be served alone or on greens.

As a variation, omit mint and add 1 red onion, sliced, and 1 green pepper, seeded and cut in 2″ julienne strips.

283

CUCUMBERS WITH YOGHURT AND FRESH HERBS
(*Middle Eastern*)

Serves 6
Doubles
Refrigerates

TIME:
about 45 minutes

The herbs must have 2 hours to "work."

You will need . . .

4 or 5 cucumbers, peeled, quartered lengthwise, cut in 1" pieces
½ cup fresh mint, chopped
1 small onion, grated
Grated rind and juice of 1 lemon
½ tsp salt
¼ tsp white pepper
1½ cups plain yoghurt

½ cup sour cream
Parsley, chopped, to taste

POTATO SALAD–MAISON (*French*)

Serves 6
Doubles
Refrigerates

TOTAL TIME:
24 hours
(for dressing to work);
preparation 1 hour

You will need . . .

½ cup olive oil
3 Tbs white vinegar
2 tsp prepared mustard
1 large clove garlic, pressed
½ tsp salt
¼ tsp white pepper
1 tsp sugar

4 or 5 good-size potatoes, boiled about 20 minutes (done, but still firm)

½ cup (at least) parsley, very finely chopped

CAESAR SALAD (*American*)

Preparation . . .

1. In large salad bowl, combine first three ingredients; toss thoroughly.
2. Add salt and pepper and anchovies (or bacon); toss thoroughly.
3. Mix oil and garlic and add to salad; toss thoroughly.
4. Add cheese; toss thoroughly.
5. Sprinkle croutons on top; serve.

Lemon juice, egg, oregano, salt, pepper, oil, garlic, and cheese may be combined in container of electric blender (at low speed for 15 seconds); if you use anchovies, add them, too, together with oil in which they are packed.

CUCUMBERS WITH ORANGES AND SOUR CREAM (*Middle Eastern*)

Preparation . . .

1. Combine these four ingredients to make dressing.
2. Combine oranges and cucumber with dressing; mix well. Chill.

   This salad may be served alone or on greens.

   As a variation, omit mint and add 1 red onion, sliced, and 1 green pepper, seeded and cut in 2" julienne strips.

CUCUMBERS WITH YOGHURT AND FRESH HERBS
(*Middle Eastern*)

Serves 6
Doubles
Refrigerates

TIME:
about 45 minutes

The herbs must have 2 hours to "work."

You will need . . .

4 or 5 cucumbers,
peeled, quartered lengthwise,
cut in 1" pieces
½ cup fresh mint, chopped
1 small onion, grated
Grated rind and juice of 1 lemon
½ tsp salt
¼ tsp white pepper
1½ cups plain yoghurt

½ cup sour cream
Parsley, chopped, to taste

POTATO SALAD–MAISON (*French*)

Serves 6
Doubles
Refrigerates

TOTAL TIME:
24 hours
(for dressing to work);
preparation 1 hour

You will need . . .

½ cup olive oil
3 Tbs white vinegar
2 tsp prepared mustard
1 large clove garlic, pressed
½ tsp salt
¼ tsp white pepper
1 tsp sugar

4 or 5 good-size potatoes,
boiled about 20 minutes
(done, but still firm)

½ cup (at least) parsley,
very finely chopped

CUCUMBERS WITH YOGHURT AND FRESH HERBS
(*Middle Eastern*)

Preparation . . .

1. Combine first seven ingredients, mix well, cover, and chill for 2 hours.
2. To serve, stir in sour cream, sprinkle with parsley.

If desired, 1 tsp prepared horseradish may be added to yoghurt; it gives a nice zip. Also, 1 tsp ground cumin is a pleasant addition.

Mint is best for seasoning the salad; but fresh dill is entirely satisfactory, with the addition of horseradish or cumin.

POTATO SALAD–MAISON (*French*)

Preparation . . .

1. In jar with tight-fitting lid, combine first seven ingredients *24 hours in advance*; shake well and let "work" in refrigerator.
2. Cool potatoes, remove skins, dice, and chill.

At this point, potatoes may be refrigerated, if well covered. Do not refrigerate overnight after dressing and potatoes are combined.

To serve, toss potatoes with dressing; chill for 1 or 2 hours, covered, to let flavors meld. Before serving, add parsley and toss again.

HOT SLAW–MAISON (*German*)

*Serves 6
Doubles*

TIME:
about 20 minutes

You will need . . .

1 egg
⅓ cup cream
1 tsp salt
1 tsp sugar
¼ tsp dry mustard
¼ tsp pepper

¾ cup vinegar, boiling

1 head young cabbage, shredded

SPINACH SALAD (*French*)

*Serves 6
Doubles*

TIME:
about 30 minutes

You will need . . .

1 lb. spinach,
washed, shaken dry; stems removed;
leaves torn to bite size

1 large bunch water cress; washed,
shaken dry; heavy stems removed

1 clove garlic
1 tsp sugar
Grated rind of 1 lemon
½ tsp salt
¼ tsp pepper
¼ tsp paprika
3 Tbs lemon juice
3 Tbs sour cream
½ cup oil

HOT SLAW—MAISON (*German*)

Preparation . . .

1. In container of electric blender combine these six ingredients and blend on low speed (15 seconds).

2. With blender running, add boiling vinegar to contents of container.
3. Pour sauce over cabbage in salad bowl; toss well.

The same dressing may be used for wilted lettuce salad, an American dish—only because, as I see it, lettuce is "American" and cabbage is "German."

SPINACH SALAD (*French*)

Preparation . . .

1. In salad bowl, toss together greens; refrigerate.

2. In container of electric blender, combine these nine ingredients; blend at low speed for 15 seconds.
3. When ready to serve, pour dressing over chilled greens and toss thoroughly.

The salad may also be served with "All-purpose" dressing, p. 278, or with the dressing for "Water Cress with Mushrooms," p. 290.

SPINACH SALAD WITH ORANGE AND BACON
(*American*)

*Serves 6
Doubles*

TOTAL TIME:
about 50 minutes

Served alone or with dessert cheese, a fine ending to any meal.

You will need . . .

1 lb. spinach,
washed, shaken dry; stems removed;
leaves torn to bite size
6 to 8 scallions, sliced
(with green tops, if crisp)

3 oranges, peeled, seeded, diced

8 slices bacon, rendered
crisp, drained, crumbled

3 Tbs reserved bacon fat
3 Tbs lemon juice
3 Tbs oil
1 Tbs sugar
½ tsp salt
1 tsp dried tarragon

SPINACH SALAD WITH ORANGE AND BACON
(*American*)

Preparation . . .

1. In salad bowl, toss together spinach and scallions; refrigerate.

2. In separate bowl, refrigerate oranges.
3. Do *not* refrigerate bacon. Reserve 3 Tbs fat.
4. In saucepan, combine these six ingredients.

At this point you may stop and continue later.

5. Bring contents of saucepan to rapid boil, stirring. Pour over greens and toss thoroughly. Add oranges and reserved bacon; toss again. Serve at once.

WATER CRESS AND MUSHROOM SALAD–MAISON
(*American*)

Serves 6
Doubles

TOTAL TIME:
about 1 hour

Make dressing 1 hour before serving. Mushrooms "drink" salad dressing at an alarming rate: toss only at moment of serving.

You will need . . .

2 bunches water cress, washed, shaken dry, heavy stems removed
½ lb. mushrooms

¼ cup oil
1 clove garlic

3 Tbs lemon juice
1 tsp sugar
½ tsp salt
¼ tsp white pepper
Herb of your choice, if desired (see p. 277)

BULGUR SALAD (*Lebanese*)

Serves 6
Doubles
Refrigerates

TOTAL TIME:
about 1¼ hours

You will need . . .

2 cups coarse bulgur
6 cups salted water, boiling

12 scallions, chopped
2 cups parsley, finely chopped
3 tomatoes, peeled, seeded, chopped
½ cup oil
Grated rind and juice of 1 lemon

Fresh mint leaves, chopped (optional)

WATER CRESS AND MUSHROOM SALAD—MAISON
(*American*)

Preparation . . .

1. Under cold water, rinse mushrooms; loosen any dirt with finger tips; cut off discolored bits; slice. Refrigerate water cress and mushrooms in sealed container.
2. Pour oil into salad bowl. Put garlic through press into oil. Let stand 1 hour.
3. In jar with tight-fitting lid, combine lemon juice with seasonings; shake well to dissolve sugar. Let stand 1 hour.
4. To serve, combine oil and lemon juice mixtures; add water cress and mushrooms; toss thoroughly.

BULGUR SALAD (*Lebanese*)

Preparation . . .

1. Cover bulgur with water and let soak until cool. Drain thoroughly, pressing out excess moisture.
2. In mixing bowl, combine bulgur with these five ingredients, tossing thoroughly with forks (to keep grains separate). If necessary, add more oil and lemon juice. Refrigerate.
3. When serving, garnish with mint, if desired.

When fresh parsley or mint is unavailable use 2 Tbs dried parsley and 2 tsp dried mint, ground in a mortar; toss with "cooked" bulgur before adding other ingredients.

A Few Breads and Muffins

The cook who wants specially to please family or friends will sometimes offer home-made bread. Remarkably easy to make, yeast breads need only a bit of time to rise, and in most cases you can bake today for tomorrow's meal—or, better, freeze until you want to serve the bread that you have made at leisure. Quick breads are as little trouble, for the dry and the liquid ingredients may be mixed separately ahead of time and combined at the moment of baking. The following recipes are appetizing changes from rice, barley, or bulgur dishes.

BOCK BEER BREAD (*German*)

1 large loaf
or
2 small loaves
Doubles
Refrigerates
Freezes

TOTAL TIME:
about 3¼ hours

You will need . . .

1 cup bock beer
2 packets dry yeast
3 Tbs brown sugar
1 tsp salt
1 egg, beaten
3 Tbs butter, melted

3 to 4 cups flour
(unbleached if possible)
½ cup wheat germ

A hearty bread goes well with beef dishes. Nobody will detect the beer, which, adding richness, does not taste. Bock beer, formerly a springtime drink, is now available most of the year; however, any dark beer (beer, not stout) will substitute.

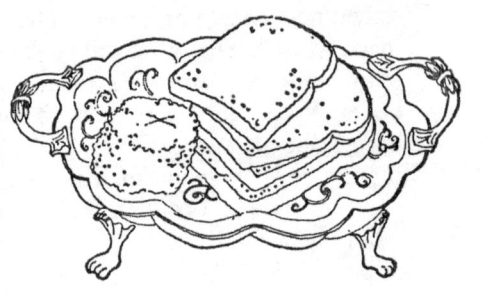

BOCK BEER BREAD (*German*)

Preparation and baking . . .

1. Heat beer until lukewarm and pour into warm bowl. Sprinkle yeast over and allow to dissolve. Add sugar, salt, and egg; stir to dissolve sugar. Add butter.

2. Mix in half the flour. Add wheat germ, stirring. Add remaining flour, turn onto floured surface, and knead.
3. Place dough ball in warm, buttered bowl and cover with a cloth; put in warm, sheltered place (I use the unheated oven); let rise until double in bulk.
4. Butter 9"x5" loaf pan, or two smaller ones, if desired. Mold dough into loaf, place in pan, and let rise again. When dough reaches just over top of pan, remove from unheated oven (assuming you have used it) and set aside until oven is heated to 375°. Bake for 30 to 40 minutes, or until bread sounds hollow when tapped on top. Let cool a few minutes, remove from pan and place on rack to cool fully.

OATMEAL-RAISIN BREAD (*American*)

2 loaves
Refrigerates
Freezes

TOTAL TIME:
about 3¼ hours

You will need . . .

2 cups old fashioned oatmeal
½ cup molasses
1 tsp salt
4 Tbs butter
2 cups water, boiling

3 packets dry yeast
½ cup lukewarm water
1 cup raisins

5 cups flour
(unbleached if possible)

GOUGÈRE (*French*)

Serves 6
Doubles

TIME:
about 1 hour

You will need . . .

1 cup water
6 Tbs butter
1 tsp salt
¼ tsp white pepper

1 cup flour
4 eggs
1 cup Gruyère or Meunster
cheese, chopped fine

Among the tastiest of quick breads, the gougère, a cheese puff from Burgundy, is easily made.

OATMEAL-RAISIN BREAD (*American*)

Preparation and baking . . .

1. In warm bowl, combine oatmeal, molasses, salt, and butter. Add water, stirring, and let stand until cool (about 15 minutes).
2. Dissolve yeast in water and add to cooled contents of bowl, stirring. Add raisins.
3. Add flour, 1 cup at a time, mixing, until dough is too heavy to stir. Turn onto floured surface, adding flour and kneading, until dough is of smooth, rubbery consistency.
4. For rising and baking, proceed as with recipe for Bock Beer Bread, p. 295. Use two 9"x5" loaf pans.

GOUGÈRE (*French*)

Preparation and baking . . .

Gougère is a *very* quick bread; preheat oven to 425° and lightly butter a large pie tin.

1. In saucepan, combine water, butter, and seasonings; heat until butter is melted and water boils steadily.
2. Add flour all at once; cook, stirring, until ball forms away from sides of pan. Remove from heat. Add eggs, singly, beating each in thoroughly. Add cheese and blend.
3. In large spoonfuls arrange dough around sides of pie tin; leave empty area in middle. Bake 40 to 45 minutes or until *gougère* is puffed and golden—like popovers. Serve at once.

BREAD EN CASSEROLE—MAISON (*French*)

2 loaves
Refrigerates
Freezes

TOTAL TIME:
about 3¼ hours

You will need . . .

2 packets dry yeast
2 cups warm water or milk
3 Tbs butter, melted
2 Tbs sugar
2 tsp salt

4 to 4½ cups flour
(unbleached if possible)

This recipe is a versatile one: in its given form the result is French; Variations I and II give it a strongly American flavor; Variation III is Italian; Variations IV and V have no native country, but very good tastes. If desired, two small loaf pans may be used in place of the casserole; the round loaves, however, in contrast to standard oblongs, add a visual interest to the meal.

BREAD EN CASSEROLE—MAISON (*French*)

Preparation and baking . . .

1. In warm bowl, dissolve yeast in water or milk. Add butter, sugar, and salt, stirring to dissolve sugar.

2. Add flour, 1 cup at a time, and mix thoroughly. Dough should be soft and sticky.
3. Cover bowl with cloth and let rise in warm place until double in bulk. Stir down and spoon into two buttered 1-quart casseroles. Cover and let rise until dough reaches top of casserole.
4. Bake at 375° for about 50 minutes, or until bread sounds hollow when tapped. Remove from casseroles and cool on rack.

    Variation I (American): mix 2 tsp dried dill weed with flour.

    Variation II (American): mix 1 Tbs instant onion with liquids and 2 tsp rubbed leaf sage with flour.

    Variation III (Italian): mix ½ cup grated Parmesan cheese and 1 Tbs (generous) dried oregano with flour.

    Variation IV: mix 1 packet onion-flavored salad-dressing mix with flour.

    Variation V: mix ¼ tsp each of nutmeg, sweet basil, and thyme with flour.

MUFFINS (*American*)

---

12 to 18 muffins
Doubles
Refrigerates
Freezes

TOTAL TIME:
about 30 minutes

You will need . . .

2 cups pastry flour
1 Tbs baking powder
½ tsp salt
2 Tbs sugar

2 eggs, beaten
1 cup milk
¼ cup butter, melted

Dry and liquid ingredients may be mixed separately and combined at the moment of baking. Muffins come in various guises, but all are variations on a basic, simple theme.

Variations

Bacon: Use 2 Tbs butter and 2 Tbs bacon fat; add to batter 3 Tbs cooked bacon, crumbled; substitute ¾ cup corn meal for 1 cup flour.

Banana: Mash thoroughly 1 banana; add to liquid ingredients.

Bran: Substitute 1 cup bran for 1 cup flour.

Cheese-bran: Use only 2 Tbs butter; add 1 cup shredded Cheddar cheese to liquid ingredients; substitute 1 cup bran for 1 cup flour.

Mushroom: Drain 1 4-oz. can mushroom stems and pieces; reserve liquid and add milk to yield 1 cup; add mushroom bits to liquid ingredients.

MUFFINS (*American*)

Preparation and baking . . .

1. Mix together dry ingredients.
2. Mix together liquid ingredients.
3. At time of baking, pour liquid over dry ingredients. Stir only enough to dampen flour. Spoon into buttered muffin tins or baking cups (about ⅔ full). Bake at 400° for 15 minutes.

Variations

Orange: Add 1 Tbs grated orange rind and (optional) ½ cup white seedless raisins to liquid ingredients.

Raisin: Add ½ cup raisins or currants to liquid ingredients.

Raisin-apple: Add ¼ cup raisins, ½ cup finely chopped raw apple, and 1 Tbs grated lemon rind to liquid ingredients; add ½ tsp powdered ginger to dry ingredients.

Spiced: Add ½ tsp ground allspice and ¼ tsp each of cinnamon and clove to dry ingredients. Or ½ tsp each of mace, clove, cinnamon, and ginger.

Whole wheat or graham: Substitute ¾ cup whole wheat or graham flour for 1 cup of white flour.

Desserts

The following recipes for desserts are of the make-ahead variety. Only one or two require a last-minute touch. The first three, for hearty desserts, are good accompaniments to soup-and-salad meals. The others are light, designed to end a meal with freshness of taste.

BLUEBERRY DUFF (*American*)

Serves 6 to 8
Doubles
Refrigerates
Freezes

TOTAL TIME:
about 1½ hours

You will need . . .

2 cups flour
1 cup sugar
4 tsp baking powder
Pinch of salt

2 eggs, beaten
½ cup vegetable oil
¼ cup milk
½ tsp lemon extract (optional)

2 cups blueberries,
washed and drained

GINGERBREAD (*American*)

Serves 8
Doubles
Refrigerates
Freezes

TOTAL TIME:
about 1 hour

You will need . . .

½ cup brown sugar
¼ cup bacon fat
¼ cup butter
1 egg, beaten
1 cup dark molasses

2½ cups bread flour
1½ tsp baking soda
1½ tsp powdered ginger
1 tsp cinnamon
½ tsp ground clove
½ tsp salt

1 cup boiling water

This recipe for old-fashioned gingerbread makes a dish substantial in itself. It is especially good served with either whipped or iced cream, or with lemon sauce, page 306.

BLUEBERRY DUFF (*American*)

Preparation and baking . . .

1. Assemble and prepare all ingredients.
2. Mix together dry ingredients.
3. Mix together liquid ingredients. Combine with dry and beat until smooth.
4. Fold in blueberries. Butter a 5"x9" loaf pan and flour it. Fill with batter and bake at 350° for 1 hour, or until cake tests done when pricked with broom-straw.

Serve with Lemon Sauce, p. 306.

GINGERBREAD (*American*)

Preparation and baking . . .

1. Assemble and prepare all ingredients.
2. Beat together until creamy sugar and shortenings. Add egg and mix thoroughly. Add molasses and mix thoroughly.
3. Mix together dry ingredients.

At this point you may stop and continue later.

4. Combine molasses and flour mixtures; add water gradually, beating to free batter of lumps. Beat about 3 minutes. Bake in buttered shallow square pan at 350° for 35 minutes, or until gingerbread tests done. Cool slightly and turn out of pan onto rack.

LEMON SAUCE FOR BLUEBERRY DUFF AND GINGERBREAD

You will need . . .

½ cup sugar
1 Tbs cornstarch
1 cup water
3 Tbs butter
Grated rind and juice of 1 lemon
Pinch of salt

RICE PUDDING (*Greek*)

Serves 6
Doubles
Refrigerates

TOTAL TIME:
about 3½ hours

You will need . . .

1 qt. milk, scalded
½ cup raw natural rice

Grated rind of 1 orange
5 Tbs honey

Cinnamon
Freshly grated nutmeg

½ cup orange juice
½ cup sugar

¼ cup Cointreau or
other orange-flavored liqueur
Grated rind of 1 orange

LEMON SAUCE FOR BLUEBERRY DUFF AND GINGERBREAD

Preparation . . .

In saucepan, combine sugar and cornstarch. Add water and cook, stirring, until mixture is thickened and clear. Add remaining ingredients and cook, stirring, until butter is melted and blended into sauce.

RICE PUDDING (*Greek*)

Preparation and cooking . . .

1. In 2- or 3-quart casserole, combine milk and rice; bake, uncovered, at 250° for 3 hours, or until rice is tender and most of liquid is absorbed.
2. After first hour, add orange rind and honey.
3. When done, dust pudding with cinnamon and nutmeg.
4. In saucepan, boil orange juice and sugar for 5 minutes.
5. Add liqueur and orange rind; simmer for 5 minutes.

Serve sauce separately.

If desired, ½ cup white seedless raisins may be added with orange rind and honey.

INDIVIDUAL CHOCOLATE MOUSSE (*French*)

*Serves 6
Doubles
Refrigerates*

TIME:
about 15 minutes

You will need . . .

1 6-oz. package semi-sweet chocolate bits
2 eggs
1 tsp vanilla
Pinch of salt

2 Tbs sugar
¾ cup milk

Easy to make, easy to serve, easy to eat! For large groups, set the mousse in 3-oz. unwaxed paper cups.

INDIVIDUAL CHOCOLATE MOUSSE (*French*)

Preparation . . .

Chocolate bits and eggs should be at room temperature.

1. In container of electric blender, combine these four ingredients.

2. In saucepan, combine sugar and milk and bring to rapid boil.
3. Pour boiling milk over ingredients in blender, simultaneously turning blender on at low speed. Cover and blend for 25 seconds, or until chocolate is melted and mixture is smooth. Pour into dishes or cups; refrigerate several hours before serving.

If desired, garnish with sprinkling of grated unsweetened chocolate.

SPONGE PUDDING—MAISON (*American*)

Serves 6
Refrigerates

TOTAL TIME:
about 30 minutes to make;
6 hours to chill

You will need . . .

2 squares bitter chocolate
½ cup water
¾ cup sugar
1 packet unflavored gelatin
softened in ¼ cup water

1 large can Carnation
evaporated milk
1 tsp vanilla

The basic recipe is for chocolate-flavored pudding, albeit I most frequently use the fruit-flavored variations.

SPONGE PUDDING—MAISON (American)

Preparation . . .

1. Assemble and prepare all ingredients.
   Evaporated milk should be refrigerated overnight, together with mixing bowl and beater.
2. In saucepan, melt chocolate in water. Add sugar and then gelatin mixture, stirring until all is melted. Cool.
3. In cold bowl, whip until stiff refrigerated evaporated milk. Stir vanilla into chocolate syrup; fold syrup into whipped milk. Chill for 6 hours before serving.

   If desired, may be served with whipped cream in large bowl or individual dishes.

   Variation I: Omit chocolate and water; increase sugar to 1 cup, use juice and grated rind of 2 lemons or 2 limes.

   Variation II: Omit chocolate and water; use ½ cup sugar, ½ cup orange juice, grated rind of 1 orange, and 4 bananas, mashed to creamy consistency.

JELLIED SHERRY (*Spanish*)

Serves 6
Doubles
Refrigerates

TOTAL TIME:
about 30 minutes to make;
6 hours to set

You will need . . .

2 packets unflavored gelatin
softened in ¼ cup cold water
1 cup boiling water
¾ cup sugar
Pinch of salt

1½ cups sherry
½ cup orange juice
2 Tbs lemon juice

DRIED FRUIT COMPOTE (*International*)

Serves 6
Doubles
Refrigerates

TIME:
about 1¼ hours

You will need . . .

1 box mixed dried fruit
1 cup raisins
3 cups water
⅓ cup sugar
Juice and peels of
1 lemon and 1 orange
3" piece cinnamon bark

Sour cream

JELLIED SHERRY (*Spanish*)

Preparation . . .

1. Assemble and prepare all ingredients.
2. In mixing bowl, add boiling water to softened gelatin; add sugar and salt and stir until all are dissolved. Cool; do not allow to set (about 15 minutes)
3. Stir in sherry and juices. Pour into mold and chill.

   Orange sections, peeled and seeded, or canned mandarin oranges may be added.

   If desired, may be served with sour cream sauce, p. 314.

DRIED FRUIT COMPOTE (*International*)

Preparation and cooking . . .

1. In baking dish with tight-fitting lid, combine all ingredients. Bake, covered, at 325° for 1 hour. Allow to cool; chill; remove peel.

2. Serve with sour cream.

COMPOTE OF KUMQUATS AND LEECHEE NUTS
(*Chinese*)

Serves 6
Doubles
Refrigerates

1 can kumquats
1 can leechee nuts
Powdered ginger

SEEDLESS GRAPES IN SOUR CREAM—MAISON
(*American*)

Serves 6
Doubles
Refrigerates

TOTAL TIME:
about 20 minutes preparation
3 hours to chill

You will need . . .

2 lbs. seedless grapes, stems removed, washed, thoroughly drained

2 cups sour cream
4 Tbs dark brown sugar
2 Tbs lemon juice

The recipe works equally well with pineapples.

Variation I: In container of electric blender, combine 2 cups sour cream, ⅓ cup maple syrup, ¼ cup cognac, 3 or 4 fresh mint leaves, chopped; blend at low speed for 10 seconds. Pour over grapes and chill.

Variation II: Blend 2 cups sour cream, ½ tsp ground cinnamon, 4 Tbs dark brown sugar, and ¼ cup Cointreau or other orange-flavored liqueur. Pour over grapes and chill.

COMPOTE OF KUMQUATS AND LEECHEE NUTS
(*Chinese*)

Combine kumquats and leechee nuts and their juices; sprinkle with ginger. Chill.

This compote, which is not offered as a "recipe," is a fitting ending to Chinese meals. Serve in small individual dishes with toothpicks.

SEEDLESS GRAPES IN SOUR CREAM–MAISON
(*American*)

Preparation . . .

Blend these three ingredients, combine with grapes, and finish with sprinkling of brown sugar; chill.

Variation III: Blend 2 cups sour cream, 2 tsp powdered ginger, 1 Tbs preserved ginger, chopped, and ⅓ cup maple syrup. Pour over grapes and chill.

If you use fresh pineapple, peel the fruit and cut the meat into bite-size pieces; proceed as with seedless grapes.

If you use canned pineapple, buy 2 20-oz. cans of pineapple chunks; drain well before adding sauce.

PEARS WITH RED WINE—MAISON (*French*)

Serves 6
Doubles
Refrigerates

TOTAL TIME:
about 20 minutes to make;
4 hours to chill

This recipe works equally well with canned peach halves.

You will need . . .

⅔ cup dry red wine
⅔ cup reserved syrup
from canned pears
8 whole cloves
3″ piece cinnamon bark
Peel of 1 lemon

1 29-oz. can Bartlett pear halves

PEARS WITH CURRY (*Middle Eastern*)

Serves 6
Doubles

TOTAL TIME:
about 30 minutes

This recipe works equally well with canned peach halves.

You will need . . .

4 Tbs soft butter
½ cup (packed) dark brown sugar
2 tsp curry powder
Pinch of salt

1 29-oz. can Bartlett pear halves

PEARS WITH RED WINE—MAISON (*French*)

Preparation . . .

1. In saucepan, combine all ingredients, bring to boil; reduce heat and simmer, covered, for 15 minutes.

2. Arrange pear halves in serving bowl; pour over them hot wine mixture. Cover and allow to cool. Chill thoroughly.

PEARS WITH CURRY (*Middle Eastern*)

Preparation and baking . . .

1. Mix together these four ingredients. Put a ball of the mixture into centers of pear halves. Arrange them on lightly buttered pie tin.

   At this point you may stop and continue at serving time.

2. Bake pears at 325° for 15 minutes.

A Few Drinks and Appetizers

Here are a few ideas for *hors d'oeuvres*—unusual appetizers which may be prepared in advance of serving—and for drinks—beverages suitable as cocktails which may also be used as accompaniment to meals.

LIVER PATÉ

Serves 6
Doubles
Refrigerates

TOTAL TIME:
30 minutes to make;
several hours to set

You will need . . .

2 cans commercial liver paté
2 3-oz. packages cream cheese

3 Tbs cognac
½ tsp each:
mace
ground clove
salt
white pepper
2 Tbs chives, minced

LIPTAUER CHEESE (*Austrian*)

Serves 6 to 8
Doubles
Refrigerates

TOTAL TIME:
about 45 minutes to make;
several hours to set

You will need . . .

1 half-pint carton cottage cheese

1 3-oz. package cream cheese
4 Tbs butter

1 tsp anchovy paste
1 small onion, grated
1½ tsp paprika
½ tsp salt
¼ tsp white pepper

Liptauer cheese, a favorite in
Vienna, is prepared 24 hours
in advance.

LIVER PATÉ

Preparation . . .

Have all ingredients at room temperature.

1. Blend together paté and cheese.
2. Add cognac, seasonings, and chives; mix thoroughly. Refrigerate in mold.
3. Before serving, remove from mold; allow to rechill.

Serve with Melba toast.

LIPTAUER CHEESE (*Austrian*)

Preparation . . .

Have all ingredients at room temperature.

1. Force cottage cheese through sieve.
2. Blend thoroughly cottage cheese, cream cheese, and butter.
3. Add seasonings and mix well. Refrigerate overnight in covered crockery or plastic bowl.

In Austria, Liptauer cheese is served as a course, just as Camembert, for example, is used in France. Try it as a cheese to accompany salad.

Serve with Melba toast, rye bread rounds, crackers, or "dip chips." The flavor is better if not served chilled: remove from refrigerator ½ hour before serving.

BABA GHANOUGE–MAISON (*Middle Eastern*)

Serves 8
Doubles
Refrigerates

TOTAL TIME:
1½ *hours to make; several hours to "work" and chill*

You will need . . .

1 large eggplant

5 Tbs *tahine* (sesame-seed purée—available at specialty and health food stores) (or 3 Tbs vegetable oil)
1 tsp salt
½ tsp pepper
¾ tsp prepared horseradish (if desired)
Grated rind and juice of 1 lemon

GUACAMOLE–MAISON (*Mexican*)

Serves 6 to 8
Doubles
Refrigerates

TIME:
about 30 minutes

This recipe is a combination of several guacamole formulae, and more flavorful, I think.

You will need . . .

3 ripe avocados

2 Tbs onion, grated
2 Tbs lemon juice
¾ tsp salt
¾ tsp chili powder
1 clove garlic, pressed
1 tomato, peeled and diced
1 dash Tabasco
½ tsp sugar

BABA GHANOUGE–MAISON (*Middle Eastern*)

Preparation . . .

1. With fork, make a few holes in eggplant. Bake on pie- or cookie-sheet at 400° for 1 hour, or until soft. Skin eggplant and put pulp in container of electric blender.
2. Add remaining ingredients and blend at low speed for 15 seconds, or until thoroughly mixed. Chill. In absence of blender, eggplant may be mashed and ingredients mixed with silver fork.

Serve with sesame-seed crackers.

GUACAMOLE–MAISON (*Mexican*)

Preparation . . .

1. Peel avocados and mash pulp in earthenware or plastic bowl with silver fork.
2. Add remaining ingredients and mix thoroughly. Chill. (To prevent discoloring when refrigerated, cover *guacamole* with plastic wrap touching directly on it.)

RAW VEGETABLES WITH GREEN MAYONNAISE (*French*)

As appetizer or side dish, raw vegetables are colorful, fresh to the palate, and satisfying. I once thought it daring to serve raw broccoli stalks; I then discovered not only broccoli stalks, but the broccoli flower as well, *and* raw mushrooms, raw beets, raw zucchini, and raw cauliflower.

The grossest, toughest broccoli stalk is more tasty raw than cooked. Cut the stalk off just below the flower and lengthwise into ¼" strips; then peel the "bark" from each strip. Keep crisp in lightly salted chilled water.

Buy clean, well-formed, medium-sized mushrooms. Rinse gently under cold

---

GREEN MAYONNAISE

About 1¼ *cups*
TIME:
about 20 *minutes*

You will need . . .
½ cup parsley, chopped
1 cup raw spinach, chopped
½ cup chives, chopped
(frozen will do)
1 egg
½ tsp salt
½ tsp dry mustard
2 Tbs wine vinegar
¼ tsp white pepper
½ tsp sugar
¼ cup oil

¾ cup oil

RAW VEGETABLES WITH GREEN MAYONNAISE (*French*)

water, rubbing lightly with finger tip to loosen dirt; cut off discolored bits. Drain well, split in half, and chill in tightly covered container.

Beets served raw should be large ones. Peel off outer skin and cut into strips of suitable size for use with dip. Serve beets separately from other vegetables for they will tint red whatever they touch.

Use young zucchini. Rinse well, remove ends, and cut lengthwise in ½" strips; cut strips in half and refrigerate.

The vegetables mentioned here—and cold boiled shrimp—are especially good with . . .

GREEN MAYONNAISE

Preparation . . .

1. In container of electric blender, combine first ten ingredients; cover and turn to low speed. Immediately . . .
2. . . . remove cover, and add remaining oil in slow, steady stream. When oil is poured, turn off blender.

CREAM CHEESE DIP (*American*)

*Serves 6 to 8
Doubles
Refrigerates*

TIME:
about 20 minutes

Another dressing for raw vegetables is this dip, also good with corn swirls, potato chips, etc. So that crackers or chips will not break, use a bit more milk.

You will need . . .

1 8-oz. package cream cheese
Milk

1 Tbs green pepper, minced
1 Tbs pimento, minced
1 small onion, grated
2 Tbs fresh parsley, minced
½ tsp salt
Dash white pepper

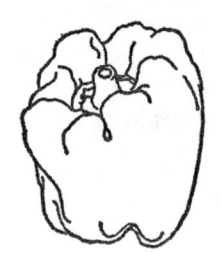

WHISKEY PUNCH

About 45 punch-glass servings

Salubrious, safe, and money-saving. Far and away my favorite for casual entertaining when supper is to be served, for it may be used as a cocktail and continued throughout the evening.

You will need . . .

1½ cups lemon juice
¾ to 1 cup sugar (to taste)
2 fifths blended whiskey
1 pint *strong* cold tea

Block of ice
2 qts. club soda, chilled

CREAM CHEESE DIP (*American*)

Preparation . . .

Have all ingredients at room temperature.

1. Blend cream cheese with milk until of desired consistency (add milk slowly, so that you do not use too much).
2. Add remaining ingredients and mix thoroughly. Chill.

WHISKEY PUNCH

Preparation . . .

1. Stir together lemon juice and sugar until sugar is dissolved. Add whiskey and tea; mix well.

   At this point you may stop and continue later.

2. In punch bowl, arrange ice block, pour over whiskey mixture; add club soda just before serving; stir gently.

FISH HOUSE PUNCH (*American*)

About 50 punch-glass servings

Fish House Punch was known to Washington and Lafayette. One story claims it to have been first made at The Fish House, an inn located on the wharves of pre-Revolutionary Philadelphia's harbor. The glamor of its legend is matched by its flavor.

You will need . . .

¾ lb. sugar
2 qts. water
1 qt. lemon juice

2 fifths dark rum
1 fifth cognac
6 ozs. peach or apricot liqueur

Block of ice

RED WINE AND CIDER PUNCH (*French*)

About 35 punch-glass servings

You will need . . .

½ gal. dry red wine
1 qt. apple cider
½ cup lemon juice
⅔ cup sugar

Block of ice
1 qt. ginger ale (optional)

FISH HOUSE PUNCH (*American*)

Preparation . . .

1. Combine these three ingredients, stirring until sugar is dissolved.
2. Add liquors and mix well.
3. In punch bowl, arrange ice; pour mixture over, stirring gently to chill well.

RED WINE AND CIDER PUNCH (*French*)

Preparation . . .

1. Combine these four ingredients, stirring to dissolve sugar.
2. In punch bowl, arrange ice; pour mixture over. Just before serving, add ginger ale and stir gently.

Apple juice may be substituted for cider.

MULLED WINE (*French*)

About 1½ quarts
Doubles

Nothing more cheery on a snappy evening. The recipe triples or quadruples as easily as it doubles.

You will need . . .

1 lemon, sliced and seeded
1 orange, sliced and seeded
⅔ cup sugar
2 cups water
1 tsp whole cloves
2 3" sticks cinnamon

1 bottle dry red wine

AFTER-DINNER DEMI-TASSE

The following variations work well with either American or espresso grinds. Flavored coffee does not take cream.

Add to container in which coffee is made:

3" stick cinnamon bark
or
6 to 8 whole cloves
or
the peel of 1 lemon
or
½ the peel of 1 orange

MULLED WINE (*French*)

Preparation . . .

1. Combine these six ingredients, bring to boil; simmer, covered, for 10 minutes.

2. Add wine and heat through, stirring gently; do not allow to boil.

Index

Main dishes are listed under the ingredients named in their title. Thus, Fish filets with white wine and cumin is also indexed as:
White wine with fish filets and cumin
and
Cumin with fish filets and white wine

Side dishes—appetizers, breads, vegetables, desserts, etc.—are listed under those specific categories as well as by name.

All recipes are cross-indexed under "Nationalities and Geographical Sources." Reference to the text will show the region or culture from which a recipe comes; in the index, listed under that source, are found other recipes from the same area or culture.

A

APPETIZERS, 319–327
   baba ghanouge, 322–323
   cream cheese dip, 326–327
   green mayonnaise with raw vegetables, 324–325
   guacamole, 322–323
   Liptauer cheese, 320–321
   liver paté, 320–321
   vegetables, raw, with green mayonnaise, 324–325
APPLES with duck, 178–179
   with sausage and cabbage, 130–131
APRICOTS with chicken and rice, 146–147
   with lamb, 58–59
   with pork, 90–91
ARTICHOKE HEARTS with chicken and peanuts, 144–145

B

BABA GHANOUGE, 322–323
BAKING DISHES, 16
BAMBOO SHOOTS with shrimp, 206–207
BARBECUED (oven-) chicken, 170–171
BARLEY, 251–255
BEANS, baked with franks, 122–123
   green, with sour cream, 266–267
   with sausage, 128–129
   with veal and sausage, 120–121
BEEF, 23–55
   brisket with vegetables, 26–27
   ground, with eggplant, 34–35
   ground, with mushrooms and sour cream, 42–43
   with beer and herbs, 24–25
   with Burgundy, 28–29
   with currants, 30–31
   with curry, 32–33
   with fruit, 36–37
   with ginger, 38–39
   with olives and rice, 44–45
   with onions, 46–47
   with paprika (goulash), 40–41
   with sauerkraut, 48–49
   with tapioca, 50–51
   with vegetables, 52–53
   with white wine and sour cream, 54–55
BEER, bock, bread, 294–295
   with beef and herbs, 24–25

Index

with pork and vegetables, 92–93
BEVERAGES (see DRINKS), 326–331
BLUEBERRY DUFF, 304–305
BOCK BEER BREAD, 294–295
BOUILLON, 15
BREADS, 293–299
  bock beer, 294–295
  en casserole, 298–299
  variations, 299
  gougère, 296–297
  muffins, 300–301
  oatmeal-raisin, 296–297
BROTHS, 15
BULGUR, 251–255
  salad, 290–291
BURGUNDY, red, with beef, 28–29
BUTTER, 15, 17
BUTTERMILK with chicken and curry, 148–149

C

CABBAGE with sausage and apples, 130–131
CAESAR SALAD, 282–283
CANNED GOODS, sizes of, 15–16
CARROTS with nutmeg and honey, 268–269
  variations, 268–269
  with tripe and onions, 136–137
CASSEROLE, type of, 12, 15, 21
CHEESE, cream, dip, 326–327
  Liptauer, 320–321
  with fish filets and sherry, 188–189
CHERRIES, maraschino, with chicken and mandarin oranges, 158–159
CHICKEN with apricots and rice, 146–147
  with artichoke hearts and peanuts, 144–145
  browning of, 143
  with curry and buttermilk, 148–149
  with figs, 150–151
  with ginger and olives, 152–153
  with lemon and sour cream, 154–155
  with lemon and tarragon, 156–157
  with mandarin oranges and maraschino cherries, 158–159
  oven-barbecued, 170–171
  oven-fried, 172–173
  with paprika, 160–161
  with prunes and sherry, 162–163
  with sherry and cream, 164–165
  with sweet wine, 166–167
  with white port and coriander, 168–169
CHICKEN LOAF, 174–175
CHOCOLATE MOUSSE, individual, 308–309
CIDER, red wine and, punch, 328–329
CLAMS with eggplant, 202–203
COD filets with shrimp and rice, 208–209
COFFEE, after-dinner, 330
  demi-tasse, 330–331
COMPOTE, dried fruit, 312–313
  of kumquats and leechee nuts, 314–315
CONDIMENTS for curries, 57
CONSOMMÉ, 15
CORIANDER with chicken and white port, 168–169
CORN OIL, 17
CRABMEAT with shrimp, 210–211, 212–213
CRANBERRIES with tongue, 134–135
CREAM with chicken and sherry, 164–165

Index

CREAM CHEESE, dip, 326-327
CUCUMBERS with oranges and sour cream, 282-283
   with yoghurt and fresh herbs, 284-285
CUMIN with fish filets and white wine, 194-195
   with lamb and sherry, 60-61
CURRANTS with beef, 30-31
CURRY, butter, 272
   condiments or side dishes for, 57
   with beef, 32-33
   with chicken and buttermilk, 148-149
   with lamb, 64-65
   with lamb, ground, and yoghurt, 86-87
   with lamb and lentils, 62-63
   with lamb and tomatoes, 66-67
   with peaches, 316-317
   with pears, 316-317
   with shrimp and mushrooms, 216-217

D

DEMI-TASSE, 330-331
DESSERTS, 303-317
   blueberry duff, 304-305
   compote, dried fruit, 312-313
   kumquats and leechee nuts, 314-315
   gingerbread, 304-305
   jellied sherry, 312-313
   lemon sauce, 306-307
   mousse, individual chocolate, 308-309
   pears with curry, 316-317
   pears with red wine, 316-317
   pineapple in sour cream, 315
   rice pudding, 306-307
   seedless grapes in sour cream, 314-315
   sponge pudding, 310-311
DOUBLING, 16

DRIED FRUIT, compote, 312-313
DRINKS, 326-331
   Fish House punch, 328-329
   mulled wine, 330-331
   red wine with cider punch, 328-329
   whiskey punch, 326-327
DUCK, browning of, 143
   with apples, 178-179
   with ginger, 180-181
   with olives and mushrooms, 182-183
DUFF, blueberry, 304-305

E

EGGPLANT, 16
   with clams, 202-203
   with ground beef, 34-35
   with ground lamb, 70-71
   with lamb chops, 72-73
   with stewed lamb, 68-69
ENDIVE, braised, 266-267

F

FIGS with chicken, 150-151
FISH FILETS, 185-195
   preparation of, 187
   with cheese and sherry, 188-189
   with orange sauce, 190-191
   with peaches and ginger, 192-193
   with vegetables, stewed, 228-229
   with white wine and cumin, 194-195
FISH HOUSE PUNCH, 328-329
FRANKS with baked beans, 122-123
FRANKFURTERS (see FRANKS)
FREEZING, 16, 21

Index

FRIED (oven-) chicken, 172–173
FROZEN INGREDIENTS, 16–17
FRUIT compote, dried, 312–313
  with beef, 36–37
  with lamb and rice, 74–75

G

GEOGRAPHICAL SOURCES (see NATIONALITIES)
GINGER with beef, 38–39
  with chicken and olives, 152–153
  with duck, 180–181
  with fish filets and peaches, 192–193
GINGERBREAD, 304–305
GOUGÈRE, 296–297
GOULASH, 40–41
GRAPES, seedless, in sour cream, 314–315
GREEN MAYONNAISE, 324–325
  with raw vegetables, 324–325
GUACAMOLE, 322–323
GUMBO, shrimp, 214–215

H

HERBS with beef and beer, 24–25
HOLLANDAISE SAUCE, 273
  "short order," 273
HOMINY with tripe, 138–139
HORS D'OEUVRES (see APPETIZERS)

I

INGREDIENTS, selection of, 12–13

J

JELLIED SHERRY, 312–313

K

KUMQUATS and leechee nuts, compote, 314–315

L

LAMB with apricots, 58–59
  with cumin and sherry, 60–61
  with curry, 64–65
  with curry and lentils, 62–63
  with curry and tomatoes, 66–67
  with eggplant, 68–69
  with fruit and rice, 74–75
  ground, with eggplant, 70–71
  ground, with yoghurt and sherry, 86–87
  with paprika, 76–77
  with parsley and lentils, 78–79
  with raisins and spices, 80–81
  with sour cherries, 82–83
  with vegetables, 84–85
LAMBCHOPS with eggplant, 72–73
LEECHEE NUTS, compote of, with kumquats, 314–315
LEMON with chicken and sour cream, 154–155
  with chicken and tarragon, 156–157
LEMON SAUCE, 306–307
LENTILS with lamb and curry, 62–63
  with lamb and parsley, 78–79
LETTUCE, wilted, salad, 286–287
LIPTAUER CHEESE, 320–321
LIVER PATÉ, 320–321
LOAF, chicken, 174–175

M

MAISON (indicating author's recipes), 11
MARGARINE, 14, 17

Index

MARINATING, 17
MAYONNAISE, 280-281
  green mayonnaise, 324-325
MEATS, 23-117
  beef, 23-55
  lamb, 57-87
  pork, 89-95
  rabbit, 97-103
  variety, 119-139
  veal, 105-117
MOUSSE, chocolate, individual, 308-309
MUFFINS, 300-301
  bacon, 300
  banana, 300
  bran, 300
  cheese-bran, 300
  mushroom, 300
  orange, 301
  raisin, 301
  raisin-apple, 301
  spiced, 301
  whole wheat, 301
MULLED WINE, 330-331
MUSHROOM and water cress salad, 290-291
MUSHROOMS with duck and olives, 182-183
  with ground beef and sour cream, 42-43
  with rabbit and sour cream, 98-99
  with shrimp and curry, 216-217
  with veal and sour cream, 114-115

N

NATIONALITIES and GEOGRAPHICAL SOURCES, explained, 12
Afghanistan: meat soup with vegetables, 238-239
Alsatian: pork with sauerkraut, 94-95

American
  appetizer: cream cheese dip, 326-327
  beans, baked, with franks, 122-123
  beef with fruit, 36-37
    with tapioca, 50-51
    with vegetables, 52-53
  bread: oatmeal-raisin, 296-297
    (see also: bread *en casserole,* 298-299)
  chicken with artichoke hearts and peanuts, 144-145
    with lemon and tarragon, 156-157
    with prunes and sherry, 162-163
  chicken loaf, 174-175
  clams with eggplant, 202-203
  desserts: blueberry duff, 304-305
    gingerbread, 304-305
    pineapple in sour cream, 314-315
    seedless grapes in sour cream, 314-315
    sponge pudding, 310-311
  drinks: Fish House punch, 328-329
  fish chowder, 240-241
  fish filets with cheese and sherry, 188-189
  lamb with sour cherries, 82-83
  muffins, 300-301
  oven-barbecued chicken, 170-171
  oven-fried chicken, 172-173
  oxtail with raisins and olives, 126-127
  rice with orange and thyme, 255
    brown, with currants and scallions, 256-257
  salads: Caesar, 282-283
    spinach with orange and bacon, 288-289

339

Index

water cress and mushroom, 290–291
wilted lettuce, 287
sausage with cabbage and apples, 130–131
seafood stew, 246–247
scallop stew, 244–245
shrimp gumbo, 214–215
shrimp with crabmeat, 210–211, 212–213
tongue with cranberries, 134–136
vegetables: green beans with sour cream, 266–267
spinach with sour cream and horseradish, 270–271
Arabian: lamb with curry and tomatoes, 66–67
Austrian
appetizer: Liptauer cheese, 320–321
chicken with paprika, 160–161
veal with paprika, 110–111
Burmese: beef with ginger, 38–39
Cambodian: fish chowder with pineapple, 242–243
Ceylonese: veal with oriental spices, 108–109
Chinese
dessert: compote of kumquats and leechee nuts, 314–315
duck with ginger, 180–181
shrimp with bamboo shoots, 206–207
sweet-and-sour, 222–223
with vegetables, 224–225
vegetables, sweet-and-sour, 264–265
Danish: pea soup, 235
Dutch
fish filets with peaches and ginger, 192–193
pea soup, 234–235
Flemish
beef with beer and herbs, 24–25

onion soup, 232–233
pork with beer and vegetables, 92–93
vegetables: carrots with nutmeg and honey, 268–269
onions with honey, 270–271
French
appetizer: raw vegetables with green mayonnaise, 324–325
beef brisket with vegetables, 26–27
with Burgundy, 28–29
breads: *en casserole,* 298–299
gougère, 296–297
desserts: individual chocolate mousse, 308–309
pears with red wine, 316–317
drinks: mulled wine, 330–331
red wine and cider punch, 328–329
duck with apples, 178–179
fish filets with orange sauce, 190–191
fish stew with vegetables, 228–229
oxtail with onions, 124–125
rabbit with orange sauce, 100–101
with red wine, 102–103
salads: potato, 284–285
spinach, 286–287
sausage with ratatouille, 132–133
soups: potato, 236–237
ham with beans and vegetables, 230–231
tripe with carrots and onions, 136–137
veal with sausage and beans, 120–121
with vegetables, 116–117
vegetables: braised endive, 266–267
braised fennel, 266–267
onions with apples, 270–271

Index

ratatouille, 262-263
German
  bread: bock beer, 294-295
  salad: hot slaw, 286-287
Greek
  beef with currants, 30-31
    with onions, 46-47
  dessert: rice pudding, 306-307
  fish filets with white wine and cumin, 194-195
  scallops with rice, 198-199
    with wine-and-cheese sauce, 200-201
Haitian
  chicken with sweet wine, 166-167
Hungarian
  beef with paprika (goulash), 40-41
    with white wine and sour cream, 54-55
  goulash, 40-41
  lamb with paprika, 76-77
  rabbit with mushrooms and sour cream, 98-99
Indian
  lamb with curry, 64-65
    with curry and lentils, 62-63
    ground, with yoghurt and curry, 86-87
Irish
  lamb with vegetables (Irish stew), 84-85
Italian
  beef, ground, with eggplant, 34-35
  lambchops with eggplant, 72-73
  pork with apricots, 90-91
  shrimp with scallops and rice, 218-219
Lebanese: bulgur salad, 290-291
Malayan
  beef with ginger, 38-39
  chicken with ginger and olives, 152-153
Mexican
  appetizer: *guacamole*, 322-323
  sausage with beans, 128-129
  tripe with hominy, 138-139
Middle Eastern (regional as opposed to national recipes)
  appetizer: *baba ghanouge*, 322-323
  beef with curry, 32-33
    ground, with olives and rice, 44-45
  chicken with apricots and rice, 146-147
    with figs, 150-151
    with mandarin orange and maraschino cherries, 158-159
  dessert: pears with curry, 316-317
  lamb with apricots, 58-59
    with eggplant, 68-69
    with fruit and rice, 74-75
  salads: cucumber with oranges and sour cream, 282-283
    cucumber with yoghurt and fresh herbs, 284-285
  shrimp with mushrooms and curry, 216-217
    with scallops and rice, 220-221
  veal with pears, 112-113
North African: lamb with raisins and spices, 80-81
Polish: beef with sauerkraut, 48-49
Portuguese: chicken with white port and coriander, 168-169
Rumanian
  chicken with lemon and sour cream, 154-155
  lamb, ground, with eggplant, 70-71
  vegetables, mixed, *en casserole*, 260-261

Index

Russian
  beef, ground, with mushrooms and sour cream, 42–43
  veal with sour cream and mushrooms, 114–115

Spanish
  chicken with sherry and cream, 164–165
  dessert: jellied sherry, 312–313
  duck with olives and mushrooms, 182–183
  lamb with cumin and sherry, 60–61
  rice with saffron and tomatoes, 256–257
  shrimp with cod filets and rice, 208–209
  veal with oranges, 106–107

Syrian
  chicken with curry and buttermilk, 148–149
  lamb with parsley and lentils, 78–79
  vegetables: zucchini with tomatoes, 272–273

O

OATMEAL-RAISIN BREAD, 296–297
OILS, corn and olive, 17
OLIVES with chicken and ginger, 152–153
  with duck and mushrooms, 182–183
  with ground beef and rice, 44–45
  with oxtail and raisins, 126–127
ONIONS with apples, 270
  with beef, 46–47
  with honey, 270–271
  with oxtail, 124–125
  with tripe and carrots, 136–137
ORANGES with veal, 106–107
  mandarin, with chicken and maraschino cherries, 158–159
ORANGE SAUCE with fish filets, 190–191
  with rabbit, 100–101
OVEN-BARBECUED CHICKEN, 170–171
OVEN COOKING, 17
OVEN-FRIED CHICKEN, 172–173
OXTAIL with onions, 124–125
  with raisins and olives, 126–127

P

PAPRIKA with beef (goulash), 40–41
  with chicken, 160–161
  with lamb, 76–77
  with veal, 110–111
PARSLEY, dried, fresh, and frozen, 18
  with lamb and lentils, 78–79
PATÉ, liver, 320–321
PEACHES with curry, 316–317
  with fish filets and ginger, 192–193
PEANUTS with chicken and artichoke hearts, 144–145
PEARS with curry, 316–317
  with red wine, 316–317
  with veal, 112–113
PEPPER, black, red, and white, 18
PINEAPPLE in sour cream, 314–315
PORK with apricots, 90–91
  with beer and vegetables, 92–93
  with sauerkraut, 94–95
PORT, white, with chicken and coriander, 168–169
POTATO SALAD, 284–285
POULTRY, chicken, 141–175
  duck, 141, 178–183

Index

PRUNES with chicken and sherry, 162–163
PUDDING, rice, 306–307
  sponge, 310–311
  variations, 311
PUNCH, Fish House, 328–329
  red wine and cider, 328–329
  whiskey, 326–327

R

RABBIT with mushrooms and sour cream, 98–99
  with orange sauce, 100–101
  with red wine, 102–103
RAISINS with lamb and spices, 80–81
  with oxtail and olives, 126–127
RATATOUILLE (see Vegetables)
  with sausage, 132–133
RAW VEGETABLES with green mayonnaise, 324–325
RED WINE and cider punch, 328–329
  with pears, 316–317
  with rabbit, 102–103
REFRIGERATING, 18, 21
RICE, 251–255
  brown, with currants and scallions, 256–257
  pudding, 306–307
  with chicken and apricots, 146–147
  with ground beef and olives, 44–45
  with lamb and fruit, 74–75
  with orange and thyme, 255
  with saffron and tomatoes, 256–257
  with scallops, 198–199
  with shrimp and cod filet, 208–209
  with shrimp and scallops, 218–219, 220–221

S

SALADS, 275–291
  bulgur, 290–291
  Caesar, 282–283
  cucumber with oranges and sour cream, 282–283
  with yoghurt and fresh herbs, 284–285
  dressing, "All-purpose," 278–279
  mayonnaise, 280–281
  slightly-sweet, 278–279
  hot slaw, 286–287
  potato, 284–285
  spinach, 286–287
  with orange and bacon, 288–289
  water cress and mushroom, 290–291
  wilted lettuce, 287
SAUCE, lemon, 306–307
  sour cream, 314–315
  for vegetables, 272–273
SAUERKRAUT with beef, 48–49
  with pork, 94–95
SAUSAGE with beans, 128–129
  with cabbage and apples, 130–131
  with ratatouille, 132–133
  with veal and beans, 120–121
SCALLOPS with rice, 198–199
  with shrimp and rice, 218–219, 220–221
  with wine-and-cheese sauce, 200–201
SEA FOOD, 185, 197–225
  clams, 202–203
  scallops, 197–201
  shrimp, 205–225
SEEDLESS GRAPES in sour cream, 314–315
SHERRY, jellied, 312–313
  with chicken and cream, 164–165

343

Index

with chicken and prunes, 162–163
with fish filets and cheese, 188–189
with lamb and cumin, 60–61
SHRIMP gumbo, 214–215
  with bamboo shoots, 206–207
  with cod filets and rice, 208–209
  with crabmeat, 210–211, 212–213
  with mushrooms and curry, 216–217
  with scallops and rice, 218–219, 220–221
  sweet-and-sour, 222–223
  with vegetables, 224–225
SLAW, hot, 286–287
SOUPS and SOUP-STEWS, 227–247
  bean with ham and vegetables, 230–231
  fish chowder, 240–241
    with pineapple, 242–243
    with vegetables, 228–229
  ham with beans and vegetables, 230–231
  meat with vegetables, 238–239
  onion, 232–233
  pea, Dutch, 234–235
    Danish, 235
  pineapple, fish chowder with, 242–243
  potato, 236–237
  scallop stew, 244–245
  seafood stew, 246–247
  vegetables, with fish, 228–229
    with ham and beans, 230–231
    with meat, 238–239
SOUR CHERRIES with lamb, 82–83
SOUR CREAM, sauce, 314–315
  with beef and white wine, 54–55

with chicken and lemon, 154–155
with ground beef and mushrooms, 42–43
with pineapple, 315
with rabbit and mushrooms, 98–99
with seedless grapes, 314–315
  variations of, 314–315
with veal and mushrooms, 114–115
SPICES with lamb and raisins, 80–81
  oriental, with veal, 108–109
SPINACH, salad, 286–287
  with orange and bacon, 288–289
  with sour cream and horseradish, 270–271
SPONGE PUDDING, 310–311
  variations, 311
STOP-AND-START preparation, 15
SWEET-AND-SOUR shrimp, 222–223
  vegetables, 264

T

TAPIOCA with beef, 50–51
TARRAGON with chicken and lemon, 156–157
TOMATOES with lamb and curry, 66–67
TONGUE with cranberries, 134–135
TOP-OF-STOVE or range cooking, 17
TRIPE with carrots and onions, 136–137
  with hominy, 138–139

V

VEAL with oranges, 106–107
  with oriental spices, 108–109

with paprika, 110–111
with pears, 112–113
with sausage and beans, 120–121
with sour cream and mushrooms, 114–115
with vegetables, 116–117
VEGETABLES, 258–267
  carrots with nutmeg and honey, 268–269
  variations, 268–269
  endive, braised, 266–267
  fennel, braised, 267
  green beans and sour cream, 266–267
  mixed, *en casserole*, 260–261
  onions with apples, 270
  onions with honey, 270–271
  ratatouille, 262–263
  raw, with green mayonnaise, 324–325
  sauces for:
    curry butter, 272
    Hollandaise, 273
    short-order "Hollandaise," 273
  spinach with sour cream and horseradish, 270–271
  sweet-and-sour, 264–265
  with beef, 52–53
  with beef brisket, 26–27
  with fish stew, 228–229
  with lamb, 82–83
  with pork and beer, 92–93
  with shrimp, 224–225
  with veal, 116–117
  zucchini with tomatoes, 272–273

W

WATER CRESS and mushroom salad, 290–291
WHISKEY PUNCH, 326–327
WILTED LETTUCE salad, 286–287
WINE, serving of, 11
  cooking with, 18
  -and-cheese sauce with scallops, 200–201
  mulled, 330–331
  sweet, with chicken, 166–167
  white, with beef and sour cream, 54–55
  white, with fish filets and cumin, 194–195

Y

YOGHURT with ground lamb and curry, 86–87

Z

ZUCCHINI with tomatoes, 272–273